Play:
Working
Partner
of Growth

Judy Spitler McKee,
Editor

ASSOCIATION FOR
CHILDHOOD EDUCATION INTERNATIONAL
11141 Georgia Avenue, Suite 200
Wheaton, MD 20902
(301) 942-2443

Photographs, front cover:
Clockwise from left—Donna J. Harris, Merrill-
Palmer Institute; Graham Bell; Sue Peterson.
Back cover:
Clockwise from top left—Shirley Eagen;
Bruce Jennings; Donna J. Harris, Merrill-
Palmer Institute.
Frontispiece, page 4:
Bruce Jennings

Lucy Prete Martin, Director of Publications/Editor
Mary N.S.W. Parker, Editorial Assistant, Special Publications

Library of Congress Cataloging-in-Publication Data
Play, working partner of growth.
  Bibliography: p. 80
  1. Play. 2. Child development. 3. Education,
Preschool. I. McKee, Judy Spitler.
LB1137.P556 1986   372'.21   86-22245
ISBN 0-87173-112-6

1986 Comprehensive Membership Order

Dedication

Play: Working Partner of Growth is dedicated to two innovative educational leaders of vision and magnanimity from Teachers College, Columbia University: Patty Smith Hill (1868-1946) and Alice Miel.

In their respective childhoods, both women freely explored the nearby woods and streams, enjoyed many playmates and displayed remarkable curiosity. Indeed, their rich playhoods prepared them for exploring new places, people and ideas throughout their lives.

Patty Smith Hill, during her Teachers College career from 1906-1935, was the articulate, forceful spokesperson for progressive programs for children and teachers. She used the emerging data of child study research and naturalistic classroom observations to defend the merits of self-selected play activities for young children. Her lifelong attempts at aligning all levels of early childhood education, to avoid insularity of teachers and discontinuity of curriculum, culminated in her heading the Department of Nursery School, Kindergarten and First-Grade Education. For more than forty years, she worked with parent education and community groups to develop culturally relevant curriculum for poor and immigrant children. Additionally, she was an active member of the International Kindergarten Union and its successor, the Association for Childhood Education.

During her tenure at Teachers College (1944-1971), **Alice Miel** demonstrated her belief that "the printed word allows a person to cross both time and space" by authoring influential books on several topics. Their titles attest to her breadth of interests and expertise: *Changing the Curriculum* (1946), *Cooperative Procedures in Learning* (1952), *More Than Social Studies* (1957), *Creativity in Teaching* (1961) and *Supervision for Improved Instruction* (1972). She has served as a consultant in schools in the United States, Puerto Rico, Japan and Afghanistan. A staunch supporter of ACEI, Alice Miel delivered the dedicatory address at the organization's Center Dedication Ceremony in 1960. Her cosmopolitan work continues during her retirement through Project Milestone, developed by her students, dedicated to advancing inquiry, research and educational practice and to fostering a sense of world community.

Both Patty Smith Hill and Alice Miel have influenced several generations of educational leaders in the United States and abroad. Today's children, families and educators owe them a debt of gratitude for their compassionate, humanitarian achievements—all of which represent an unswerving commitment to curriculum reform and democratic learning processes.

Foreword

Play to the child is growth—
the gaining of life. *Joseph Lee*

Childhood is Playhood. *A.S. Neill*

Lee's 1915 view remains valid today. Research evidence has rapidly accumulated for more than two decades on identifying the elusive, complex and profound ways that children's play represents their individual growth, development and learning about the physical, emotional, social, intellectual, creative and sociocultural facets of their world.

Neill's view that "Childhood is Playhood" enjoys less acceptance today. Recent scholarly treatises have been written on *The Hurried Child* (Elkind, 1981) and *The Erosion of Childhood* (Suransky, 1982). Today, more and more stressed children have less and less time, space and materials for play and fewer, helpful adults who encourage their playful pursuits or are available or willing to engage in play partnerships with them. Concerned adults report on increasing numbers of children who do not and cannot play constructively due to malnutrition, neglect, overwhelming anxieties, unrealistic adult expectations, perfectionism, severe handicaps, or crises such as family separation, divorce or abuse. Yet, researchers, clinicians, educators and humane parents concur that all children need play as a working partner in their childhood to ensure their healthy, harmonious and happy development.

As programs for young children have become more highly structured and adult-centered, and as more parents expect early instruction and formal academic activities for young children, early childhood educators at all levels have to be able to resist such hazardous, growth-inhibiting pressures and persuasively defend the developmental, educational and therapeutic uses of play in their programs.

The backgrounds of the authors in this publication are interdisciplinary, representing early childhood education, developmental and educational psychology, playground research, nursing and social work. The authors have tried to be both helpful and playful in their writing, intending that the readers could become more playful partners with children and more knowledgeable and helpful in legitimating play's unique value in education, family life and childhood. They believe, along with Neill, that childhood is—and should be—playhood.

Another group of experts who are knowledgeable about play and its purposes deserve our reflective consideration, also. They are our young children.*

Boy, age 4:   "Play, play, umm. Play is Play Dough."
Boy, age 4½: "Play is the big blocks. They're the best fun. We slide outside."
Boy, age 5:   "Play is funner. Funner than anything!"*
Girl, age 5½: "Play is fun and about friends. Play is about friends most."

*Interviews on play's meaning and values were conducted with several hundred children. The most common response from children ranging in age from 4 to 11 years was "Play is funner!"

Girl, age 6:	"Play is reading *The Three Bears*. We play three bears in kindergarten with our teacher. We need three beds and three bears everytime we play."
Girl, age 6½:	"Play is the best thing in the whole wide world. Don't ever let grownups ever, ever take away play from children!"
Girl, age 6½:	"Play is listening to records and singing at school."
Girl, age 7:	"Play is just fun. You get the giggles out. We laugh, too."
Girl, age 7½:	"Play is writing on the chalkboard. Play is writing in my journal with pictures I draw. Let me think. We write stories about playtime."
Boy, age 8:	"Play, uum. When you're playing, you're just looking for adventure—and you find it in play."
Girl, age 8½:	"Play is what God gave little children to make them happy."
Girl, age 9:	"Sometimes I play house with my dolls. I learn how to take care of babies. So when I am older, I will know how to be a mother."
Boy, age 9½:	"Play is doing what you want. When no one bosses you, that's play. Your way is play way."
Boy, age 10:	"Play is about two things for me. It's either playing an instrument, or it's going out on the playground. No, three things. It's also going up in the classroom and doing the work I like—math games and Clue and Chess, especially."

In their childlike ways, these children have lucidly and vividly explicated for adults the varied and unique ways that play is their working partner of growth.

Judy Spitler McKee, Editor

References

Elkind, D. *The Hurried Child*. Boston: Addison-Wesley, 1981.
Lee, J. *Play in Education*. New York: Macmillan, 1915.
Neill, A. S. *Summerhill*. New York: Hart, 1960.
Suransky, V. P. *The Erosion of Childhood*. Chicago: University of Chicago Press, 1982.

ABOUT THE EDITOR

Judy Spitler McKee is Professor of Educational Psychology/Early Childhood Education at Eastern Michigan University, Ypsilanti. She has taught and served as consultant for nursery school, day care, Head Start, kindergarten, Title I and 1st-grade programs. Dr. McKee is actively involved in early childhood education on the international, national, state and local levels. Her consultations include the areas of assessment, Piaget, play, curriculum and stress-reduction for children in crisis. Her publications include eight volumes of Annual Editions: Early Childhood Education (Dushkin, 1976-1987).

Contents

Make-Believe Play and Learning

Dorothy G. Singer

Dorothy G. Singer is co-author of Make-Believe *(1985) and* A Piaget Primer: How a Child Thinks *(1978). She is Professor of Psychology at University of Bridgeport, Research Affiliate of the Child Study Center at Yale University, and Co-Director of the Yale University Family Television Research and Consultation Center.*

> I observe that every child demonstrates a comprehensive curiosity. Children are interested in everything and are forever embarrassing their specialized parents by the wholeness of their interests. Children demonstrate right from the beginning that their genes are organized to help them to apprehend, comprehend, coordinate, and employ—in all directions.
>
> *Buckminster Fuller*

Children will indeed learn about the environment if they are given the opportunity to engage in what Jean Piaget called "symbolic play" (Piaget, 1962). Although Piaget attempted to make a distinction between games of make-believe and construction games, they are part of a continuum. For example, a "house" may be a place under a card table or a "house" may be constructed of blocks or even built with carpentry tools. Piaget believed that construction games formed the transition from practice games, symbolic games and games with rules to what he called adaptive behaviors (Piaget, 1962). Construction games "indicate an internal transformation of the symbolic notion towards adapted representation" (Piaget, 1962, p. 113). For example, the child who uses a piece of wood for a boat during symbolic or make-believe play may progress as he or she develops skills to the construction of an actual toy boat with masts, sails and seats. Piaget asks, as many researchers do, whether or not the actual construction of the toy boat is a "game, imitation or spontaneous work." He concludes that constructional games are at a position half-way between play and intelligent work, or between play and imitation. The idea of the boat, however, can exist in the child's mind long before the child is capable of accurately reproducing it. This aspect of childhood, the ability to use substitute objects to represent things that are unavailable, is what makes children's play creative and conducive to learning.

Unfortunately, there are some educators and parents who see "play" as a waste of time and who believe that it is possible to improve upon the genetic endowment of their children through early cognitive training. One program,

the *Better Baby Program* run by Glenn Doman in Philadelphia, enrolls babies as young as 8 months of age. These infants are exposed to flash cards with words or dots as precursors to math and reading exercises (Moore, 1984). Although Doman has described a child who learned to play a violin at age 3 and a child of 4 who can translate Japanese and French, there is *no* cited evidence in the vast child development literature that suggests that such early training has significant positive effects on a child's intelligence in later years.

Educators such as David Elkind (1981), Neil Postman (1982) and Marie Winn (1983) have lamented the loss of childhood and the need on the part of parents to transform their children into carbon copies of themselves. Postman claims that children no longer engage in the kind of games that English historians Peter and Iona Opie have catalogued in their important book on children's folklore and games. Television is blamed in part for the reduction of time children spend both in play and reading. Countries such as Japan and China use television (especially *Sesame Street* in Japan) to teach children to read while still in preschool.

Even computers have been urged upon children in the early grades (Papert, 1980) and many parents of elementary school children have enrolled their children in computer camps during the summer months. I am not advocating that we ignore the new technologies and methods of instruction, but I am suggesting a balance of play and learning especially in the preschool and early years of education. In our desperation to hop on the superbaby bandwagon, some of us may forget about the importance of play as a vehicle for learning and the continued value of the ''as if'' or playful attitude throughout our lives.

9

Benefits of Play

Piaget has delineated four kinds of play: *sensory-motor, practice play, symbolic play* and *games with rules*. Although benefits can be derived from all forms of play, it is my intent in this article to emphasize the positive aspects of *symbolic play* for learning. The benefits of play have been described fully elsewhere (Singer, 1973; Singer and Singer, 1981; Singer and Revenson, 1978; Singer and Singer, 1985), thus I will briefly summarize some of the main points. Obviously children who are involved in both sensory-motor and practice play are *improving motor skills*, both fine and gross motor coordination. The baby who waves a rattle or reaches for a mobile hanging over the crib begins to perfect his or her aim through trial and error. The child who rides a tricycle or learns to pump on the swing is developing gross motor skills. But practice games and especially symbolic or make-believe play will give a child additional opportunities for *turn-taking, sharing* and *rule-making*. Children can learn *ordering, sequencing,* how to *delay gratification*. Surely a child about to play a game of "pirates" needs some prior preparation before the game can begin. Toy boats need to be assembled; a clay island, perhaps, must be made. Odds and ends of scrap material or bottle tops go into a small box for buried treasure. Costumes and props consisting of pirate hats, eye patches, bandanas and boats are made ready and each child needs an assigned role before the game begins. Thus the game needs its rituals that develop into a script for a child. Ordering and sequencing of events are learned through the delights of a game rather than through a cognitive task.

Make-believe play increases children's *vocabulary and ability to express themselves*. Work by Fein et al. (1975), Nicholich (1977) and Saltz and Johnson (1974) suggest that pretend-play leads to language production and comprehension. Saltz and Dixon (1982) have found that training children to play-act sentences increased their retention for the sentences compared to children who used visual imagery or motor acts unrelated to the sentence. It seems reasonable that children who play "store," "house," "space-ship" need words to express their play actions, and because they are using the words in an active way, they are bound to internalize the meanings. This active stance seems important in light of the amount of television viewing of preschoolers. If parents mediated through explanation and discussion as children viewed a program, more would be learned. The number "4" flashed on the TV screen and repeated during a *Sesame Street* program would be learned more rapidly if the viewer actually handled four objects such as blocks, dolls, cups or spoons in make-believe play.

Elizabeth Skarakis (Note 1) suggests that children who are language disabled could benefit from "play" as part of the total treatment program. Introducing an approach that develops a child's representational abilities (i.e., feeding and grooming a doll), using modeling techniques and conventional play strategies, a lexicon could be mapped onto the child's activities. Through observation of play, the teacher could begin to assess whether or not the child had deficits in representational imagery as well as in language.

When children play, they tend to smile more and evidence more *positive affect* (Lieberman, 1977; Singer and Singer, 1981). Although Brainerd (1982) questions the benefits of play as a "key source of cognitive development in early childhood" (p. 118), he admits that "dramatic play may be an appropriate choice for promoting social competence, emotional development and the general well-being of the preschool child" (p. 128). It seems apparent that these benefits must surely outweigh the lack of what he calls "robust" results in play-training experiments on affective perspective or conservation of quantity.

Indeed, numerous researchers have found evidence for affective perspective in studies of socio-dramatic and social-fantasy play. The pioneering work of Smilansky (1968) in Israel demonstrated that play training led to increased gains in *creative, intellectual* and *social skills* of disadvantaged children. Connolly and Doyle (1984) found in a study of 91 children from middle and lower middle class backgrounds that those children who used the most complex fantasy transformations showed greater maturity in *affective role-taking skills*. Children were assessed through teacher ratings and observation techniques. Competence measures included teacher ratings of social competence, popularity and social role-taking skills. Children who engaged in frequent social fantasy play were more socially skilled in peer and activity-oriented classroom behavior than children who played fantasy games less frequently.

Finally, play will enable a child to use all *sense modalities* in the fullest way possible. Tasting, smelling, touching, hearing, seeing can all be heightened through play. Stroking a piece of velvet on a princess doll's cloak, imitating sounds of animals, pretend cooking and baking allow a child to learn discriminations among the senses and how to label these processes correctly.

Sex Differences in Play

In recent years, there has been some shifting on the part of girls to play with the more traditionally masculine toys; fewer boys, however, are moving into the female arena playing such games as "house," "school," "cooking" or "dress-up" (Macoby, 1980; Singer and Singer, 1981; Singer and Singer, 1985; Sutton-Smith, 1979). Children by the age of 3 or 4 are fairly consistent in their choice of play patterns. Some prefer more imaginative, pretend games, while others tend to choose more motor or practice kinds of play (Singer, Singer and Sherrod, 1980). Sex differences in play styles have been observed among different social classes and cultures. Generally, boys are more aggressive in their play choosing games of adventure, conflict and daring, while girls tend to play games that foster nurturance. Greta Fein et al. (1975) found, for example, that by 18 to 24 months girls are already feeding their toy dolls or animals. Goldberg and Lewis (1969) found that, as early as 13 months, girls will stay closer to their mothers and explore less than boys and display finer motor coordination.

Lever (1976), describing sex differences in the way *older children* play, suggests that they learn different skills from their games. Boys, for example, play games that require more role differentiation, interdependance of players, rule specifications, team formations, larger spaces and more outdoors. Girls play games that involve turn-taking in ordered sequence, choral activity, songs, rhymes, competition that is indirect, and more emphasis on developing empathy for a particular person. Boys are being socialized to prepare for the more complex roles in society, while girls are being prepared for roles that involve intimacy and affiliation, the behaviors needed in familial interactions.

In one study (Sprafkin, Serbin and Elman, 1982) researchers observed preschool boys over a 3-month period during free play in their classrooms. They found that the boys who engaged in more typically masculine games with large blocks, tools, cars, Tinker Toys, Lego and who ran and shouted and had more physical contact with other children were also rated as more aggressive and defiant by teachers on the Kohn and Rosman Symptom Checklist and Social Competence Scale. The researchers are aware that one of the reasons for this correlation is the fact that teachers may provide little supervision for male-preferred activities during free play, thus allowing more active and potentially disruptive behavior to occur. Nevertheless, the studies have found that a positive relationship between male-sex-typed activities and visual-spatial problem-solving skills does exist (Connor and Serbin, 1977). It may be that playing with the toys and being physically active is not harmful in itself, but the kind of supervision that is employed is a key factor. In our own work, for example, we found that children who ran around a room imitating Superman or Batman eventually did become disruptive (Singer and Singer, 1976), but if a teacher intervened and channeled the game into a constructive activity (building a Superman Planet or Batman City), the children's behavior became more socialized.

Shmukler (1984) also found in her work in South Africa that, when a mother structured a play situation for a child and provided some input in the form of play suggestions, stories, ideas and then stepped aside allowing the child "psychological" space, the child played more imaginatively than when mothers continuously intervened. Work by Weininger (1983) substantiates Shmukler's research. He found that highly educated women were less likely to intrude on their infant's play, but supported the course of the infant's play through interpretative comments as opposed to offering directions in a play situation involving teaching concepts to a child while using a shaped box. During free play this kind of mother also used nonverbal means to direct her infant's attention. Older mothers in the study, regardless of education, tended to be more intrusive in their child's play. Thus, a balance seems necessary in the preschool setting for the production of imaginative play. A teacher should not try to interfere too frequently during free play, but should provide stimuli or ideas conducive to imaginative development if children seem unable to get a game started, or if children begin to get over-stimulated and wild in the course of their play.

The Play Setting

Pretend play reflects a child's schemas about his or her world. Through role-playing, through use, exploration and transformation of numerous objects, through the "scripting" of the story-line, a child begins to form a microcosm of the adult world and begins to internalize the roles and expectations of society. Dina Feitelson (1979) summarizes the ingredients needed to stimulate symbolic play. Children will engage in make-believe play if there is time for such play. Studies suggest that preschoolers are spending about 3½ to 4 hours per day watching television and that time for play is becoming shortened. Play for older children has become more restricted to indoor board and card games and video games. Children are spending more time acquiring symbolic information with a resulting decrease in outdoor play and play equipment (Leeds, 1976; Sutton-Smith, 1979). In some cultures, play is even considered "frivolous" or "unworthy behavior" (Feitelson, 1979). In societies where adult responsibilities are given to children at an early age, time for play is rare.

Space is another factor needed to foster imaginative play. Even with ample physical space, such as the Manus children had (Mead, 1930), socio-dramatic play was not in evidence. According to Feitelson, space becomes "effective play space" only when it is ceded to children for this purpose. A crowded bedroom with no play area is not conducive to play, but the child who is allotted one corner of the room or even a small table could begin to use the space and know anything left there was his or hers. Family attitudes, sanction and atmosphere are necessary ingredients in determining whether or not a child will have both physical and psychological space. In this "sacred space," a game can be repeated, a necessity for mastery. Toys or arrangements can be used again and again in the play space, allowing a child rehearsal time to develop a play theme until the child feels competent.

Finally, some *play objects* are necessary as facilitators for play (Singer, 1973; Singer and Singer, 1985; Vigotsky, 1966). In one study (Daus, Note 2), an object as simple as a broken part of a toy or even a stick was enough to start a play episode. In another study (Pulaski, 1973), it was found that unstructured toys were utilized by children for longer play periods than structured ones.

A child who learns to play and develops a playful behavioral style will perhaps display the "bubbling effervescence" that Lieberman (1977) has reported in her studies of children and adolescents. The studies on adults that have looked at "playfulness" as a style suggest a strong factor called surgency/pleasure/play which includes such descriptions as "jocular," "cheerful," "enthusiastic," "smiles often," "colorful personality" and "stimulating" (Meehl et al., 1971). It may be that continued encouragement of make-believe play throughout life, whether in the form of actual toys and games of the child or fantasy and mind play of the adult, will prove to be necessary tools for more lively and interesting experiences.

Notes

[1]Skarakis, E. "The Development of Symbolic Play: Application to Assessment and Remediation of Language Disabled Children." Unpublished manuscript. Hearing and Speech Clinic, Children's Hospital of Los Angeles, Los Angeles, CA 90054, 1979.

[2]Daus, I. "The Development of Play in Groups of Kibbutz Children." Unpublished manuscript (trans. by D. Feitelson), 1969.

References

Brainerd, C.J. "Effects of Group and Individualized Dramatic Play Training on Cognitive Development." In D. J. Pepler and K. H. Rubin, eds., *The Play of Children: Current Theory and Research*, Vol. 6 of *Contributions to Human Development* Series, pp. 114-129. Basel, Switzerland: Karger, 1982.

Connolly, J. A., and Doyle, A. "Relation of Social Fantasy Play to Social Competence in Preschoolers." *Developmental Psychology* 20, 5 (1984): 797-806.

Connor, J.M., and Serbin, T.A. "Behaviorally Based Masculine and Feminine Activity Preference Scales for Preschoolers: Correlates with Other Classroom Behaviors and Cognitive Tests." *Child Development* 48 (1977): 1411-16.

Elkind, D. *The Hurried Child*. Boston: Addison-Wesley, 1981.

Fein, G., Johnson, D., Kosson, N., Stark, S., and Wasserman, L. "Sex Stereotypes and Preference in the Toy Choices of 20-month-old Boys and Girls." *Developmental Psychology* 11 (1981): 527-28.

Feitelson, D.S. "Imaginative Play and the Educational Process." In S.L. Katz, ed., *Proceedings, International Year of the Child: Child Advocacy*. Yale Child Study Center, Yale University, 1979, pp. 185-97.

Fuller, B. *Approaching the Benign Environment.* University, AL: University of Alabama Press, 1970.

Goldberg, S., and Lewis, M. "Play Behavior in the Year-Old Infant: Early Sex Differences." *Child Development* 40 (1969): 21-32.

Leeds, W. *The Toy Market.* Manuscript Folklore Archives, Logan Hall, University of Pennsylvania, 1976.

Lever, J. "Sex Differences in the Games Children Play." *Social Problems* 23 (1976): 478-87.

Lieberman, J.N. *Playfulness.* New York: Academic Press, 1977.

Maccoby, E.E. *Social Development.* New York: Harcourt, 1980.

Mead, M. *Growing Up in New Guinea.* New York: Morrow, 1930.

Meehl, P.E., Lykken, D.T., Schofield, W., and Tellegan, A. "Recaptured-Item-Technique (RIT): A Method for Reducing Somewhat the Subjective Element in Factor Naming." *Journal of Experimental Research in Personality* 5 (1971): 171-90.

Moore, G. "The Superbaby Myth." *Psychology Today* 18, 6 (1984): 6-7.

Nicholich, L.M. "Beyond Sensorimotor Intelligence: Assessment of Symbolic Maturity Through Analysis of Pretend Play." *Merrill-Palmer Quarterly* 23, 2 (1977): 89-99.

Papert, S. *Mindstorms.* New York: Basic Books, 1980.

Piaget, J. *Play, Dreams, and Imitation in Childhood.* New York: Norton, 1962.

Postman, N. *The Disappearance of Childhood.* New York: Delacorte, 1982.

Pulaski, M.A.S. "Toys and Imaginative Play." In J. Singer, ed., *The Child's World of Make-believe.* New York: Academic Press, 1973.

Saltz, E., and Johnson, J. "Training for Thematic-Fantasy Play in Culturally Disadvantaged Children: Preliminary Results." *Journal of Educational Psychology* 66, 4 (1974): 623-30.

Saltz, E., and Dixon, D. "Let's Pretend: The Role of Motoric Imagery in Memory for Sentences and Words." *Journal of Experimental Psychology* 34 (1982): 77-92.

Shmukler, D. "Imaginative Play: Its Implications for the Process of Education." In A. Sheikh, ed., *Imagery and the Educational Process.* New York: Baywood, 1984.

Singer, D.G., and Revenson, R.A. *A Piaget Primer: How a Child Thinks.* New York: New American Library, 1978.

Singer, D.G., and Singer, J.L. *Make-Believe: Games and Activities To Foster Imaginative Play in Young Children.* Glenview, IL: Scott, Foresman, 1985.

Singer, J.L. *The Child's World of Make-Believe: Experimental Studies of Imaginative Play.* New York: Academic Press, 1973.

Singer, J.L., and Singer, D.G. "Can TV Stimulate Imaginative Play?" *Journal of Communication* 26 (1976): 74-80.

Singer, J.L., and Singer, D.G. *Television, Imagination and Aggression: A Study of Preschoolers.* New Jersey: Erlbaum, 1981.

Singer, J.L., Singer, D.G., and Sherrod, L. "A Factor Analytic Study of Preschoolers' Play Behavior." *Academic Psychology Bulletin* 2 (1980): 143-56.

Smilansky, S. *The Effects of Sociodramatic Play on Disadvantaged Preschool Children.* New York: Wiley, 1968.

Sprafkin, C., Serbin, L., and Elman, M. "Sex-typing of Play and Psychological Adjustment in Young Children: An Empirical Investigation." *Journal of Abnormal Child Psychology* 10, 4 (1982): 559-67.

Sutton-Smith, B. "The Play of Girls." In C.B. Kopp and M. Kirkpatrick, eds., *Becoming Female: Perspectives on Development.* New York: Plenum, 1979, pp. 229-57.

Vygotsky, L.S. "Play and Its Role in the Mental Development of the Child." Reprinted in J.S. Bruner, A. Jolly and K. Sylva, eds., *Play: Its Role in Development and Evolution.* England: Penguin Books, 1976.

Weininger, O. "Play of Mothers with Babies: Some Relationships Between Maternal Personality and Early Attachment and Development Processes." *Psychological Reports* 53 (1983): 27-42.

Winn, M. *Children Without Childhood.* New York: Pantheon, 1983.

Thinking, Playing and Language Learning: An All-in-Fun Approach with Young Children

Judy Spitler McKee

Judy Spitler Mckee is the editor of several volumes on Early Childhood Education (1976-1987) and Professor of Early Childhood Education and Educational Psychology at Eastern Michigan University. She teaches specialized courses devoted to play and Piaget.

There is no better play material in the world than words. They surround us, go with us through our work-a-day tasks, their sound is always in our ears, their rhythms on our tongue. . . . But when we turn . . . to hearing and seeing children, to whom all the world is as play material, who think and feel through play, can we not then drop our adult utilitarian speech and listen and watch for the patterns of words and ideas? Can we not care for the *way* we say things to them and not merely *what* we say? Can we not speak in rhythm, in pleasing sounds, even in song for the mere sensuous delight it gives us and them, even though it adds nothing to the content of our remark? If we can, I feel sure children will not lose their native use of words: more, I think those of six and seven and eight who have lost it in part . . . will win back their spontaneous joy in the play of words. *Lucy Sprague Mitchell*

> All around the cobbler's bench,
> The monkey chased the weasel.
> The monkey thought 'twas all in fun.
> Pop goes the weasel!

Bruner, a cognitive psychologist, summarizing two decades of research on children's language in the U.S. and Great Britain, has stated that while language is innate to human beings, language must be nurtured through try-out and experience to be mastered. Moreover, a child's "mother tongue is most rapidly mastered when situated in playful activities" rather than the duress of striving for goals (1983, p. 65). Knowledgeable adults have noted that healthy children talk spontaneously and fluently when they are secure, absorbed in an activity, and when the adults significant to them "come alive." When there is mutual adult-child engrossment in a chosen activity, reciprocal conversation flows.

15

The best and preferred medium for "alive" or vivid interpersonal exchanges is play. Clearly, thinking, play and language are a dynamic, interrelated trio, and they appear together in "all-in-fun" situations.

Garvey (1977) has shown the multiple ways in which communication is central to play, how language and play interact to produce widening levels of competence. Researchers have shown how the most complicated grammatical and pragmatic (conversational) forms of language are initiated in play (Pellegrini, 1983; Pellegrini and Galda, 1984; Bruner, 1983). And Piaget, the Swiss scholar of cognitive research (1969; 1977), has explicated the intimate linkage between language and play, both representational forms of intelligence difficult to define or study in isolation or in the laboratory. Chukovsky (1963) collected samples of Russian children's play with language itself, which validated how they joyfully explored and manipulated sounds, words and phrases as if they were play materials with innumerable possibilities for forming and reforming, combining and re-combining, ordering and reordering, adding and deleting parts from wholes.

CHARACTERISTICS AND CIRCUMSTANCES OF PLAY

Play, manifold in form and variety, has been studied by researchers for decades; some of the circumstances under which it occurs and some of its elusive characteristics have been identified. For our purposes, those circumstances and characteristics related to children's thinking, play and language include: Attitude, Control, Relaxation, Absorption and Vivification.

When children and adults have an ATTITUDE of playfulness, failure or fear of consequences is suspended; the players are free to feel, think, do or say whatever they want in the play arena. Play is cherished by the world's children because it is voluntary, SELF-CONTROLLED. They choose whether to play or not, with whom, with what, where, how and how long. As Sutton-Smith (1979) has pointed out, this is a reversal of most of life when we are controlled by others, or when we engage in activities of necessity rather than desire or choice.

RELAXATION of mood is necessary since the player must feel some inner security and competence in the situation. This explains why children new to a program often do not play with the materials, or why distressed or abused children cannot play. But when play occurs, whether it is individual or social, construction or social-dramatic in form, an ABSORPTION occurs; the player is not easily distracted from the engrossing play.

While researchers in many countries have quibbled about what *is* and what *is not* play, playing children, *oblivious* to any of the aforementioned circumscribing aspects or characteristics, tell us simply and profoundly why they play and what immediate benefits they derive: Play is Fun. As several hundred surveyed children ages 4 to 10 years indicated to adults: "Play is funner. Play is funner than anything." Sutton-Smith argues that the vividness and excitement of play, the FUN part, is the VIVIFICATION effect. The thrill, the fun, the natural "high" that can be psychomotor, affective, cognitive and/or aesthetic may be short-lived—as when a child spends an hour raking leaves in order to jump joyously into them for ten seconds. Children around the world play for the vividness, the fun-ness, the thrilling-ness of play—and so do many early childhood educators who say they teach because they "simply love" their work with children.

PLAY AND LEARNING

How play correlates to learning is a question that has been asked by philosophers, historians, researchers, educators and parents; their respective answers vary with the perspective on play with which they originated their investigations. Theorists and researchers in the areas of child development, cognition, and social and behavioral learning have shown us that human learning occurs most readily through active, investigative, experiential and cooperative interactions with the world (Piaget, 1977; Bruner, 1962; Erikson, 1963). Play permits all of these and, without the child's intent or knowledge, produces a FUNdamental understanding about the inner self ("in here") and the outer world ("out there"). Moreover, because play is pleasurable and failure-free, the child is able to move from the personal nucleus of the self that regulates all experiences to non-self (others). The child's expressive interpretations—movement, play, laughter, music and art—are interdependent with conceptual and language abilities. Thus, one area such as play stimulates and elaborates the other such as language (Piaget, 1969; 1977).

In summary, thinking, play and language—along with movement, laughter, music and art—are primary ways the young child symbolizes the outer world; tests and modifies its form, functions and meanings, and grows in curiosity and competence. Adults and children who take delight in each other's play and language will "come alive" for each other. Let us recall Mitchell's observation that "There is no better play material in the world than words," as Chukovsky's vignettes reveal. How can playful adults, able to surrender some control to children and experience vivification in return, become "partners in play" (Singer and Singer, 1977) with children from 2 through 10 years—enabling them to delight in sounds, words, phrases and meanings so they will benefit from using language as free-play materials to be endlessly explored? Let us be mindful that an "all-in-fun" approach, like the monkey in the song, releases and develops children's thinking, play and language.

THE TODDLER STAGE: 1½ TO 3 YEARS

Play Patterns

Healthy toddlers are busy, energetic people, who have a passion to explore their physical and social surroundings in their attempts to order them. Ironically, their ceaseless attempts at ordering their world on their terms look like disorder to adults; for instance, when they rearrange and cart away food left out for eating. They delight in "fill-and-dump" play, tirelessly carting materials from one place to another, filling up containers and then dumping them out. Their play is solitary and, gradually, parallel or side by side with other children who may share the same space and materials such as blocks or sand, but without sharing of ideas. Sensory-motor play enjoyed during babyhood continues. Around 18 to 24 months, healthy children achieve a cognitive milestone in beginning to use the symbolic function (Piaget, 1969; 1977), which is manifested in language, symbolic play, deferred (remembered) imitation and art. Now the toddler is able to store direct, vivid, immediate experiences of daily living in cognitive schema—similar to a mental filing system—and later translate them into another highly personal form wherein something (e.g., a blanket, pan, doll, scribble or a few words) is used to stand for something else (e.g., an image, memory, animal, person or story fragment).

Their gradually emerging attempts to order and control their world are reflected most clearly in their *locomotor* and *language skills*, areas where action and thinking are linked and where playful adults can assist this stage child. Toddlers who are mastering locomotor skills play with *space*: they tirelessly scoot, tumble, climb up, slide down, crawl around, run, swing, roll, jump, leap or rock. They fall into laundry baskets, boxes and wastebaskets. Language is facilitated as adults talk with them and they joyously play with *sounds* and *words*, giving them much-desired *control* over their environment. They delight in *repeating names* (K-Mart), *animal noises, silly sounds*, especially those associated with toilet-training (poo poo, pee pee, kaka); *chants* (Row, row; Ashes, all fall down; chinney, chin chin; Fuzzy Wuzzy was a bear); and *jingles* (Plop, plop, fizz, fizz). Adults can assist toddlers as they engage in these exploratory and play activities by bathing them in a pleasant stream of language as they care for and play with them. Three types of conversation useful for building language performance are:

1. *Descriptions*: "What big shoes you are wearing!" "My, what a large purse you are carrying!" Many songs and stories popular with this age use this format, such as "Mary wore her red dress..." or *The Three Little Pigs*.
2. *Simple questions* involving where or who: "Where is your dolly today?" "Whose shoes are these under the bed? Are these Care Bear's shoes?" Questions involving motivation and purpose, the *why* type, are generally too cognitively complex for toddlers.
3. *Expansion* (to adult grammatical form) and *extension* (to add new information): Model the correct grammatical forms to children's language, but do *not* correct their grammar at this stage since this stops the flow. For instance, when a toddler states, "Fro truk," you can respond in a natural voice and expand the form: "Yes, you did throw the truck, a long way." You can provide extension by offering more information for the child to assimilate: "Let's pick up the truck now from the driveway. Elizabeth will be coming home soon, and she might hit your truck with her bicycle."

Let Fluency Precede Accuracy

At all levels of expression in the symbolic function—language, symbolic play, deferred imitation and art—children's fluency (flow) of production precedes their accuracy of execution. By nature, children are both young and inexperienced. Adults who demand precision in any of the symbolic forms greatly inhibit the child's spontaneous and playful productions. Preoccupation with accuracy—to "say it right" or "draw it right," or to play the story in a certain way—moves the adult from mediating at children's level of proficiency to trying to instruct them in becoming more adult. When the situation becomes work-like and controlled by the adult, the child may feel tense or insecure, and play exits the situation. If we corrected a child's early eating habits or early attempts at drawing or singing (as some adults correct children's speech and language productions), most children would not eat or draw or sing in our presence— and many do not. Instead, we should offer supportive, encouraging feedback in a playful mood rather than only corrective, accuracy-laden feedback.

Movement Activities

Toddlers enjoy simple movement chants. Three of their favorites are "Ring A-round a Rosey," "Pop Goes the Weasel" and "Motor Boat," which have the reverse actions of falling down and popping up, moving slowly and moving fast. Examine the words and you will see that the actions are the same that toddlers are engaged in as they explore and try to understand the complex concepts of *space* and *cause and effect*:

1. Ring a-round a rosey. Pocket full of posies. Ashes, ashes. We all fall down!
2. All around the cobbler's bench. The monkey chased the weasel. The monkey thought 'twas all in fun. Pop goes the weasel!
3. Motor boat, motor boat. Goes so fast. Motor boat, motor boat. Step on the gas!

Of course, the parts that cause the greatest anticipation, laughing, and cognitive and affective thrill (vivification) are the ending lines: "We all fall down," "Pop goes the weasel" and "Step on the gas." Adults who make playful fun of these simple movement chants are assisting the twin symbolic functions of symbolic play and language to burst forth in individual ways. Favorite play materials of toddlers are the push-and-pull variety that are accompanied by clacking and sounds, such as popcorn poppers, lawn mowers, push-downs, pop-up figures, and animals on moveable legs (dogs, penguins).

Musical Activities

Adults working with toddlers note their favorite songs are often rhymes with an action component. For example, "Clap, clap. Clap your hands. Clap your hands together." This can be varied to "Stamp your feet," "Shake your head," "Tap your knees" or "Roll your arms" (Oppenheim, 1984, p. 50). These are the forerunner of a beloved early childhood song requested even by 8-year-olds: "If you're happy and you know it, clap your hands." Other musical favorites include "Row, Row Your Boat" (which older children can sing as a round), "Jingle Bells," "Are You Sleeping?," "I'm a Little Teapot," and "Where Is Thumbkin?" (Bayless and Ramsey, 1982).

Depending on the maturity of the children, the adults will do most of the singing and movements, but this is critically important for modeling effects. After all, no human baby plays "Peek-a-Boo," "Hear-a-Boo," "Hide and Find Me," "This Little Piggy" or "Pat-a-Cake" unless a playful, responsive and often clown-ful adult initiates these bodily and social games with them. Issues associated with autonomy and control by others make "Five Little Monkeys" and "Taking a Bath" especially rewarding for toddlers, who must feel controlled by everyone around them:

1. Five little monkeys, jumping on a bed. One fell off and bumped his head. Mama called the doctor. The doctor said, "No more monkeys jumping on the bed!"
2. Every night I take a bath. I scrub and rub and rub. Every night I take a bath. I splash around the tub. Every night I take a bath. Face, nose, and ears. Arms and hands and legs and feet. Enough to last for years. (Bayless and Ramsey, 1982, p. 45)

Another favorite of toddlers is:

Two Little Blackbirds. Sitting on a hill. One named Jack, and one named Jill. Fly away, Jack. Fly away, Jill. Come back, Jack. Come back, Jill.

Books

Books popular with toddlers include *The Three Bears, Three Little Pigs* and *Three Little Kittens* (with varying voices), *The ABC Bunny* (Gag), *Goodnight Moon* (Brown), and Dr. Seuss's *Hop on Pop* and *One Fish Two Fish Red Fish Blue Fish*. Other books replete with language play are *Hand, Hand, Fingers, Thumb* (Perkins), *The Berenstains' B Book* (Berenstains) and *Fox in Socks* (Seuss). Speech pathologists report that "wonderful noises" children like to repeat are found in *Gobble, Growl, Grunt* (Spier) and *Mr. Brown Can Moo! Can You?* (Seuss).

Healthy toddlers exhibit great energy, curiosity and exploratory drives, and they laugh a lot. Accordingly, the adults who work with them need to possess adult levels of energy, curiosity and exploratory drives, and be able to laugh a lot so they can enjoy the children's playful pursuits and assist them for the purposes of growth.

THE PLAY STAGE: 3-7 YEARS

Play Patterns

Erik Erikson (1963) calls the period from 3 to 7 years the Play Stage where there is intimate linkage of thinking, play and language, and where pretending and "as-if" play are more readily observed. Play is now more clearly "creating model situations . . . to master reality by experiment and planning" (Erikson, 1963, p. 222). There is greater variety in children's use of materials and media, as well as a movement from purely random to more systematic approaches. Play can still be solitary but parallel, associative and cooperative forms (with shared rules and roles) can appear, indicating the exceptional importance of adapting to the many rule systems set by adults. Hence, inventing your own rules in play and getting others to follow them become a developmental milestone (Sutton-Smith, 1981).

The types of play that predominate at this stage are sensory-motor, continuing since babyhood, and symbolic play, continuing since toddlerhood. Richer, more elaborated content appears in play vignettes and is associated with home, school or medical themes; and there is more detail and discussion over construction projects with blocks or home settings. More children can sing and dance to music or carry on telephone conversations with unseen listeners.

Astute child care workers and kindergarten teachers have long noted that the children who possess the best oral language skills and social play skills generally seem the most "ready" for the next educational experience. Children of this stage who have poor expressive language and cannot play for any sustained amount of time often lack other readiness skills. Again, the linkage among thinking, language and play is apparent.

Movement Activities

Favorite finger plays and movement exercises enjoyed at earlier ages can still be used; children do not become bored with "There Was a Little Turtle" or

20

"Where Is Thumbkin" at 4 just because they knew them at 3 years. Now, clapping hand rhythms can be added for older children, first by saying, then singing, then hand-clapping them. Two favorites are:

1. Mary Mack, mack, mack. All dressed in black, black, black. With silver buttons, buttons, buttons. All down her back, back, back.
2. Say, say my playmate. I cannot play with you. My dolly has the flu. Boo, hoo, boo, hoo, hoo, hoo.

Many simple chants and rhymes can be made more complicated in rhythm patterns, which again builds awareness of language qualities and possibilities. For example, "Hickory, Dickory Dock" is a favorite of this stage, but older children can be divided so that one group recites the rhyme while the other group recites "Tick Tock" in rhythm.

Musical Activities

Songs with clear beats, rhyme, movement and repetition continue to be popular: "Row, Row Your Boat"; "Are You Sleeping?"; "Mary Had a Little Lamb"; "Twinkle, Twinkle Little Star"; "If You're Happy"; "Wheels on the Bus"; "Puff, the Magic Dragon"; "This Old Man" ("Knick, knack, paddy whack" is pure word play). "Frosty, the Snowman," "Jingle Bells," "Rudolph, the Red-Nosed Reindeer" and "Happy Birthday" (written by Mildred and Patty Hill) are requested regardless of the weather or status of birthdays. More language-mature children may add playful phrases such as "Tingo, Lingo, Mingo" to "Bingo," or "He Had a Care Bear" to "Old MacDonald." This then requires the talents of the adult to continue the "all-in-fun" singing and exploring activity and to add similar variations. Children can now be exposed to ascending and descending scale songs such as "Five Little Monkeys," earlier enjoyed as a movement and finger play. Some will want to substitute other animals such as donkeys or puppies, thus learning the enormous variability of language as well as demonstrating knowledge of syntax and semantics (word order and meaning).

Directions during transition times can be happily sung to the children: "Time to put your toys away. Safe to play another time. Clean-up time." "Goodbye, boys and girls. We had a playful day. I'll see you tomorrow." Children can be taught simple dances such as the Cha-Cha, with a rhythm of 1-2, 1-2-3, 1-2 or car-rots, broc-co-li, cabb-age. The Bunny Hop can be hilariously modified to The Froggy Jump or Doggy Scratch. In the Hokey Pokey, children become literally and figuratively absorbed in putting their "whole" selves "in" the doing, which is what we want them to do with thinking, play and language. Songs with dramatization possibilities and musical changes in loudness, softness and voice intonations—such as "The Old Gray Cat" is (creep-ing, sleep-ing)— are favorites with kindergartners.

Books

Dr. Seuss stories and other stories with repetitive phrases, silly-sounding words and voice changes enable children to anticipate, repeat and memorize the story elements, building the foundations for later re-enactments in social-dramatic play and reading (Pellegrini, 1983). A surprising number of adults have reported that the first book they think they were able to "read" was either *Hop on Pop* or *One Fish Two Fish Red Fish Blue Fish*, both by Seuss. If reading is, among other things, bringing enjoyment, engagement and expansive mean-

— Jim Cronk, Photographic Illustrations

ing to the printed words of others, then those adults had playful adults, either at home or in early childhood programs, who encouraged them to enjoy the selections many, many times. At the end of *Hop on Pop* are the "beau-tee-ful" sounding *Timbuktu* and *Constantinople*, enjoyed by word lovers of all ages. *Green Eggs and Ham* (Seuss), *The Three Bears* and *Three Little Kittens* are favorites, as are the language pictures found in *The Three Billy Goats Gruff*, *The Pokey Little Puppy* (Lowrey) and *The Nonsense Alphabet* (Lear). Children delight in the repetitive line from Gag's *Millions of Cats*: "Cats here, cats there. Cats and kittens everywhere. Hundreds of cats, thousands of cats. Millions and billions and trillions of cats."

Children can re-enact nonverbally and verbally their favorite stories in small groups, if provided with the encouragement, modeling and appropriate props such as head coverings or colored clothing, masks and simple block enclosures to simulate a setting. These can be re-enacted many times or re-told with the aid of flannel board figures, which builds both self-confidence and language competence. To maintain an *attitude* of play, a *relaxation* of mood and the child's internal *control*, plus *fun*, children should not be required to practice the stories under adult direction for productions for other children or adults. The play spirit vanishes under such duress. Many children delight in Silverstein's poem, "Boa Constrictor." This can be followed up with books such as *Crictor* (Ungerer). Coody reports that kindergarten children used the following adjectives to describe Crictor: "curvey, wiggly, slitherly, long, coiled, colorful, beautiful, and graceful" (1983, p.73).

Play Props

The provision of judiciously selected play props can spark interest, engagement and elaborations of play and language. For instance, a nursery school teacher compiled a "Three Bears Play Kit" for a child with low language skills. She included several storybooks on bears, homemade and purchased bear puppets, a tape recording of *The Three Bears*, small bowls and furniture, a "bear costume" made from a brown terry towel, two different flannel boards, and felt and laminated figures as well as art materials to draw, cut, paste and color. After several playful explorations with the Three Bears Play Kit, the child's self-esteem noticeably improved, his language was more fluent, and he asked to keep the kit so he could "read" to his family.

A gifted kindergarten teacher very successfully adapted for language production the "tent" or "blanket" type of play that children have engaged in for generations. She created a four-side red felt covering for a card table that included a door flap, a window and several velcro strips on each side for adding felt props. She added felt and realistic props for: (a) a post office with envelopes and postal box signs; (b) a gas station with plastic hoses and gas signs and prices; (c) a fire station with hats and hoses; (d) a McDonald's restaurant with yellow sponge fries, hats and paper food containers. She tested the materials over a period of weeks in several kindergartens where children had scored low on earlier language testing. Without exception, all the children talked when they used the highly stimulating materials. Many talked fluently for lengthy periods of time. During play with the fire station props, some kindergartners created their own "burn center" play episodes.

23

Topsy-Turvey Talking

As Chukovsky has shown in his research (1963), children love topsy-turveys, indicating they comprehend the "sense" of the situation and its embedded meaning or they could not invert it or transform it into "nonsense." The poem "Eletephony" (Richards) is enjoyed because of its mixed-up words. Mention to children that you would like to sing "Rudolf, the green-eared reindeer," or that "purple means stop and brown means go"; note who corrects you when you comment on the "humongous old shoes you have on today." During transition times, notice the responses to: "Let's put on your mittens for outside. Give me your toes, now." Or, "Lunchtime, everyone wash their paws!" Two gifted speech pathologists reported they used this topsy-turvey approach to help language-delayed children feel in control of the situation, laughing at the adult's errors and speaking naturally in the process.

Research on Early Childhood Activities
and Language Usage

The views of Symbolic Interaction writers such as Dewey (1933) and Mead (1934), that humans grow and develop their abilities through widening social interaction experiences, have been shown to be valid by contemporary researchers (Geneshi and DePaola, 1982; Ross, 1983; Almy, 1984). Observers of early childhood programs and classrooms often report that the two most popular play areas generate both the greatest social interaction (social-dramatic) play and accompanying social usage of language (person-to-person communication). These are the home and family centers and the constructional materials centers (blocks).

In both the home and family and the constructional materials centers, children are required by the dictates of time, space, materials and the presence of peers to become engaged, cooperate, compete, squabble and negotiate very complex social-cognitive rules, roles and plots. Recall the characteristics and circumstances of play. Immersed in the situations of home and family or constructional materials, the children can control the variable uses of the materials, decide on playmates and the use of space. Much time is spent in those areas talking about play (meta play) and social relationships. For example, "I'm mother, you're the baby! *No coffee* for you!" The astute adult hears much bantering and negotiating for identity and power, or what researchers call "social cognition" (see Chafel article). The implications are clear: thinking, play and language grow with expanding social-dramatic engagements and with partner play (Singer and Singer, 1977). Thus, home and family centers and constructional materials centers are absolutely indispensable for dramatic (solitary) and social-dramatic play interactions that allow higher levels of thinking, play and language to blossom. Unfortunately, as programs for the Play Stage child become more highly structured, formal and adult-controlled, children are provided less time, space and materials for enjoyable engagements that build the templates for developmental readiness. Or, as one 2nd-grader angrily told a kindergarten neighbor:"Stay in kindergarten! Don't go to 1st grade. First and 2nd grade is awful. All we do is work, work, work. We never get outta our seats. It's awful!"

THE WORK STAGE: 7-10 YEARS

Play and Game Patterns

Children 7 to 10 years (and to 11) are identified by Erikson (1951) as being in the Work Stage, when work habits, school accomplishments and the learning of cultural literacy become central to a child's psychosocial well-being.[1] The play of children 7 to 10 years changes from "pure" play to more time spent on *interplay* since children are increasingly more social; and games with rules set by other persons become an important yardstick for measuring one's competency and popularity. Board games, card games, games of skill (tag, ball games, jump rope) and games of strategy (checkers, Tic Tac Toe, team sports) become favorite pastimes. Solitary play takes the forms of reading for pleasure, collections, and arts and crafts, each of which requires persistence, concentration and self-discipline, which are necessary for schoolwork and the learning of work and study skills. Friends and after-school gatherings assume a key role as social-dramatic play centers on family, school, power and morality themes. As children arduously master—and many do not—new social roles and expectations, they often tattle on those who do not. Teachers who provided a picture or three-dimensional model of a robot named "Beepo," for 1st- and 2nd-graders "to tattle to," reported many children talked fluently to Beepo and then were able to return to their "seatwork" without disturbing others or wasting work time.

The Work Stage child has much more skill: psychomotor, social, cognitive and academic. The child is generally more reasonable (able to reason out things) and is able to be instructed in school information. Very often, however, while this Work Stage child is more mature in thinking, play and language, elementary classrooms are basically teacher-controlled, teacher-talk dominated, highly structured and *quiet*—with time blocks for required school work but not for play. Many observers report that 1st-, 2nd- and 3rd-grade children can no longer talk or play with other children or exercise thinking skills other than memorization. An intelligent prescription for elementary school classrooms—based on research on growth, development and learning—would be to *continue* providing the enjoyable, engaging, expanding and skill-building activities and materials of play and games. Such play and games approaches are an investment in the child's present and future growth.

Musical Activities

Children's most requested songs can be continued with zest, such as "Bingo" and "Old MacDonald." Useful additions with language play include: "I Know an Old Lady Who Swallowed a Fly," "I've Been Working on the Railroad," "Erie Canal," "I Love the Mountains," "The Mocking Bird" and "The Fox Went Out on a Starlit Night."

The Cruciality of Double Meanings

The learning of double meanings is a vital social and cognitive learning for this stage child (Sutton-Smith, 1981). Children need to be assisted by playful

[1]Erikson (1951, 1963) refers to the period from 7-11 years as the Industry (accomplishment) vs. Inferiority stage. For our purposes, the period from 7-10 will be used since this is the upper end of the Early Childhood Era.

adult partners to create their own (a) riddles that deal with word meanings and (b) secret languages that deal with letter meanings.

Dinosaur tales and riddles are much loved, partially due to the beauty and power of the names: Brontosaurus, Tyrannosaurus Rex. So, change children's names—and yours, also—to a dinosaur name, or to the name of another current play material. For instance, Christopherosaurus, Aliciaosaurus, Care Bear Jose, Care Bear Tomika. Recall that an earlier generation of children delighted in learning to say, sing and spell Supercalifragilisticexpialidocious.

Word play and word games are a natural adventure and occur in the "riddles, jokes, puns, double meanings, multiple meanings, rhymes, sound fun, and word games" children of this stage use in conversing with each other (Tomkins and Tway, 1985, p. 361). Favorite children's literature that is built on word and concept play includes: *Amelia Bedelia* (Parish), *A Cholocate Moose for Dinner* (Gwynne) and *The King Who Rained* (Gwynne), *Morris and Boris* (Wiseman), *Otter Nonsense* (Juster) and *Daffy Dictionary* (Rosenbloom).

Home and Family and Constructional Materials Centers

Since professionals have observed that the greatest quantitative and qualitative language fluency occurs in the home and family centers and the constructional materials (blocks) centers, which invite social interactive play and language, these two centers are irreplaceable in value for school-age children. The centers may have to be modified in form depending upon the constraints of the 1st, 2nd and 3rd grades. A group of adventuresome teachers in the elementary grades, who had been taught how to make systematic observations of their students at play and how to select and evaluate play materials, carefully added either a home and family center or a constructional materials center to their individual classrooms. Each reported greater student persistence to academic tasks and fewer behavioral and social problems. Teachers of compensatory education and learning disabled students who experimented by adding these centers to their programs reported similar findings, as well as improved study skills. The teachers found that play themes occurring in the home and family centers indicated a consolidation of acquired language and academic learnings as children explored confusing changes in their home and school relationships (such as divorce, separation and school failure). Some children preferred to continue "working" on a block construction over several days as it changed form and function. Again, the linkage of thinking, play and language is observable to adults when a complicated space center, airport or metropolitan park system is built and modified within the classroom setting.

Language Centers

Jokes and riddles about pickles, monsters, elephants, gorillas, salamanders, mice and moose abound in healthy children's language exchanges. Knowledgeable teachers can capitalize upon these to promote language curiosity and competence. A creative 2nd-grade teacher had her students create their own booklets based on the theme of double meanings, using the format of Gwynne's *The King Who Rained* and *A Chocolate Moose for Dinner.* The project lasted all year, and students' language understanding and achievement test scores grew. Another playful 2nd-grade teacher overheard her students telling moose jokes. She included a joke-telling time each day, and they quickly began to create their own responses. For example, "What does a moose have for breakfast?": Moose juice, moose eggs, moose toast, moose flakes, moose oatmeal. During successive weeks, mice and gorilla jokes were used. In each of these instances, the children were playing with the enormous (enormoose) flexibility and variability of thinking and language, something that takes a lifetime to master.

Poetry, a daily *must* for this stage child, can be selected from potent sources. Leland B. Jacobs, Langston Hughes, Louise Binder Scott, Shel Silverstein and Ogden Nash are beloved mesmerizers of children.

An area of the classroom can be designated a "Joke Center," "Linger, Laugh and Learn Location," "Rib-Tickler Spot" or "Collections of Funny Stuff."

Books

Books with cartoon characters will promote enjoyment as well as language expansion and concept attainment; moreover, they can inspire reluctant children to read and more able children to create other language, jokes, stories and poetry. Books based on family fun and animal happenings include: *Peanuts, Snoopy, Garfield, Marmaduke, Heathcliffe* and *The Family Circus*. Favorite books that can be read aloud and used for journal artwork and compositional writing include the *Ramona* series (Cleary), *Charlotte's Web* (White) and *The Jungle Book* (Kipling). The possibilities are limited only by the playful vision of the teachers.

SUMMARY

Adults who are playful and love language and its beauty, power, elegance and flexibility have innumerable opportunities to help young children grow in language fluency, enjoyment and competence by linking people, play and the production of sounds, words and concepts. Whether you are working with children in the Toddler Stage (1 ½ to 3 years), the Play Stage (3-7 years) or the Work Stage (7-10 years), remember:

- Bathe children in a pleasant, rhymical stream of language while engaged in everyday tasks, routines and transitions: Scrub and Rub time in the Tub!
- Model playful attitudes and actions for growing children. Surrender some control and gain enjoyment and vivification.
- Provide less corrective criticism, which blocks free expression, and more supportive feedback.
- Help young children fall in love with sounds and words and phrases: "Fuzzy Wuzzy was a bear."
- Link the self-expressive arts of movement, play, language, music and art. Do the Cha-Cha with language. Put your "whole self" in.
- Use playful interchanges: "Five Little Monkeys," topsy-turvey talk.
- Use playful songs children ask to sing over and over: "If You're Happy," "Old MacDonald."
- Select children's literature that has beautiful, repetitive, silly or elegant language: Dr. Seuss, Leland B. Jacobs or Shel Silverstein.

- Arrange play centers or language arts centers that spark higher levels of thinking, play and language: home centers, construction materials centers, joke and riddle areas.
- Include rhymes, chants, riddles and jokes that are lovely to the ear, delicious to the palate, tickling to the torso and generative to the emerging mind.

Researchers studying language for two decades in varying countries and settings have shown that it is critical that young children have accepting, responsive, playful adults who help them try out language, who model correct forms and who expand and extend their language, provide play activities and materials, and enjoy language possibilities with them. In serving as playful models, appreciative listeners, play partners and extenders, we encourage children's thinking, play and language in their manifold forms and limitless variations.[2]

References

Almy, A. "A Child's Right to Play." *Childhood Education* 60 (1984): 350.

Bayless, K.M., and Ramsey, M.W. *Music: A Way of Life for the Young Child.* St. Louis, MO: Mosby, 1982.

Bruner, J.S. *The Process of Education.* Cambridge, MA: Harvard University Press, 1962.

_____. "Play, Thought, and Language." *Peabody Journal of Education* 60 (1983): 60-69.

Coody, B. *Using Literature with Young Children* (3rd ed.). Dubuque, IA: Brown, 1983.

Chukovsky, K. *From Two to Five.* Berkeley, CA: University of California Press, 1963.

Dewey, J. *How We Think.* Boston: D.C. Heath, 1933.

Erikson, E.H. "A Healthy Personality for Every Child." Mid-Century White House Conference on Children and Youth, 1951.

_____. *Childhood and Society.* New York: Norton, 1963.

Garvey, C. *Play.* Cambridge, MA: Harvard University Press, 1977.

Genishi, C., and DiPaola, M. "Learning Through Argument in a Preschool." In L.C. Wilkinson, ed., *Communicating in the Classroom.* New York: Academic Press, 1982.

Gruber, H.E., and Vonèche, J.J. *The Essential Piaget.* New York: Basic, 1977.

Hutt, C. "Exploration and Play." In B. Sutton-Smith, ed., *Play and Learning.* New York: Gardner, 1979.

Mead, G.H. *Mind, Self and Society.* Chicago: University of Chicago Press, 1934.

Mitchell, L.S. *The Here and Now Story Book.* New York: Dutton, 1948.

Oppenheim, J.F. *Kids and Play.* New York: Ballantine, 1984.

Piaget, J., and Inhelder, B. *The Psychology of the Child.* New York: Basic, 1969.

Pellegrini, A.D., DeStefano, J.S., and Thompson, D.L. "Saying What You Mean: Using Play To Teach 'Literate Language.'" *Language Arts* 60 (1983): 380-84.

Ross, D.D. "Competence, Relational Status and Identity Work: A Study of the Social Interactions of Young Children." Paper presented at Annual Conference of National Association for the Education of Young Children, Washington, D.C., 1983.

Singer, D.G., and Singer, J.L. *Partners in Play.* New York: Harper and Row, 1977.

Sutton-Smith, B., ed. *Play and Learning.* New York: Gardner, 1979.

_____. "Play Isn't Just Kid's Stuff." Reprinted in J.S. McKee, ed., *Early Childhood Education, 80/81.* Guilford, CT: Dushkin, 1981.

Tompkins, G.E., and Tway, E. "Adventuring with Words: Keeping Language Curiosity Alive in Elementary School Children." *Childhood Education* 61 (1985): 361-65.

[2]Why did Judy the Moose dislike typing? She made so many moose-takes.

Children Play—
Children Learn

Rita Swedlow

Rita Swedlow is Associate Professor of Education at Queens College, The City University of New York. She is co-author of Early Childhood Education: A Guide for Observation and Participation *(1980) and* Young Children: Exploring and Learning *(1985).*

In Ms. Jensen's early childhood classroom, children were playing with many kinds of materials. There was woodworking and water play. Some children were manipulating clay or dough while others looked at books. Several children were in the block area.

After arranging four long blocks to form a square, Aaron moved one of them and said, "I'm parking cars." Michelle answered, "I made a big store," and Aaron promptly added, "Mine can be the parking lot, but they'll have to pay. It costs ten cents."

Pushing a stack of blocks along the floor, Jason stopped in front of Michelle's store. "I'm delivering stuff." "OK," said Michelle, "leave it here." At the other side of the block area, Annette was busily building a house.

Inez was painting at the easel. She outlined a square and painted a triangle on top for a roof. Then she added a rectangular chimney. Near the house, she painted a lollipop-type tree. In the left-hand corner of the paper she placed a big sun. In front of the house she added four flowers in a row.

On the other side of the easel, Vernon was working on quite a different picture. He was having fun painting thick vertical lines at almost equal intervals across the page, using the broad side of his brush. He paused to examine his picture. Then he placed wavy lines between the straight ones. He stopped again before placing dots between each of the waves on the page (Figure 1).

Figure 1

These activities are examples of many that were taking place in the classroom. Even a casual observer would have been aware that the children were having fun. It is easy, however, to miss the learnings that take place because adults seldom associate learning with these types of play activities. If only adults who are so eager for children to master knowledge and skills at an early age could recognize that the learnings children acquire as they play are basic to all future learning!

Learnings

Let us examine what learnings might have been taking place as Aaron, Michelle, Jason and Annette played with blocks. Each child was involved in some type of classification. Aaron and Jason classified blocks according to size. Aaron used blocks for each side of his parking lot while Jason used smaller ones, all of the same size, for the merchandise he was delivering. Michelle ran out of double unit blocks and after several tries found that two units were equivalent to a double unit. This helped her complete the wall of her structure. Annette matched blocks as she built a wall on either side of her house. After many tries, she became more aware of the similarities and differences in the size of the blocks and was able to discriminate the units, double units and quadruple unit blocks more easily.

As the children were building, they handled three-dimensional shapes and, in using them, created their own shapes. Even though Aaron did not identify it as a square, he constructed one as he made his parking lot. Michelle worked hard aligning the blocks to make a long narrow building, unaware that she was constructing a rectangle.

As Aaron parked the cars (½ column blocks) in his garage, he would step back from time to time to examine the arrangement, and he would rearrange them until he had achieved a symmetrical pattern.

In building their different structures, each child had to solve many real problems. Aaron had trouble fitting the corners of his garage together. Creating an entrance for the cars was almost an unsolvable problem for him, but he did find a solution. Annette tried several ways of making windows for her house and, after many unsuccessful tries, finished her building without them. Anyone watching Vernon at the easel would have seen him deliberately creating equal spaces between vertical lines, estimating the distance between the lines and carefully matching the thickness of each line. When he made a wavy line between the vertical lines, he created a new pattern. Vernon seemed satisfied with the symmetry and balance of his picture when he said, "I'm finished."

Inez painted two simple shapes for her representation of a house. The circle on top of a thick vertical line symbolized a tree. When she completed her picture, there was a definite configuration of shapes on the page. The figures of the tree, sun, house and flowers clearly stood out against the background of the paper. Inez was faced with a problem when the paint dripped while she was making the sun. The problem was quickly solved by transforming the drip into a ray of the sun. This was so pleasing to her that she made several more rays around her sun.

As Inez and Vernon applied paint to paper, they each held the brush in a different way. Inez seemed able to hold it with confidence, while Vernon kept changing the position of his hand on the brush attempting to achieve better control. They were not only practicing eye-hand coordination, but they were developing the skills needed for writing with a pencil.

These learnings might not seem very significant to the untrained observer, but concrete experience with shapes provides background for recognizing and using them on an abstract level as numerals, letters and sentences.

When children stack blocks, they do not necessarily count them using number words, but they are developing a sense of quantity. While they are not formally dealing with equivalencies, they are adding and subtracting as they match blocks to build a wall. After children create their own shapes with paint and brush, shapes have more meaning for them. When they have made their own representations, it is easier for them to understand and appreciate the representations of others. Children who work on their own problems become interested in problem-solving and skilled in the processes involved.

Not only do children develop intellectually as they use materials such as blocks and paint, but they develop physically, as well. There is opportunity to increase both gross and fine motor control as they manipulate objects. Aligning blocks or applying paint to paper with a brush requires eye-hand coordination, which becomes more refined with practice.

Children gain social skills as they find the need to share both materials and space with others. When they attempt to work together, it becomes necessary for them to develop their communication skills.

Children become interested in exploring and excited by their individual discoveries. They have enough success in their experiences so that failures are not devastating. Therefore, they are willing to take risks.

Imagination is nurtured as children plan personal, meaningful projects and set their own goals. As they become more competent and confident, their work becomes increasingly complex, and they develop a better self-concept.

Materials and Media

While many of the learnings and values described have been acquired through blockbuilding and brush-painting, the same learnings may be achieved through other media such as sand, water, clay, dough, wood, paste and crayons. A child can have very positive experiences in school, acquire many of these learnings, and yet not use every one of these materials.

Why are such learnings important? The attitudes, values and skills that children gain help them develop not only a depth of understanding that gives meaning to formal learning, but also a concept of themselves as learning persons.

In a democratic society, it is important for children to develop the learning processes needed for making intelligent decisions for themselves and their groups. According to John Dewey, democratic living can be learned only in action, particularly in social interaction with peers, and not through memorization, slogans or passive pursuits (Dewey, 1916; 1938).

Materials that can be used in many ways are particularly conducive to fostering these learnings. Such materials are often described as open-ended. Children are able to play with them as they wish, thus allowing imaginations to flourish. The more ways a material can be used, the more interesting it is to the children.

As children pat, pound, squeeze and roll clay, they can make long snake-like shapes, which they lay side by side, matching lengths. They can line them up around the edge of the table, pat the coils into a plate or bend the edges up to make a basket. They can make balls that may be put together to form more complex figures such as a snowman or apples in a basket.

No matter how interesting materials are, however, children will not gain the maximum benefits from them unless appropriate arrangements are made for their use. Materials need to be clean, in good repair and safe for children. They have to be easily accessible so that children can use them when they wish. When woodworking tools are displayed on a pegboard at a child's eye level, the child can get a hammer and put it back where it belongs, too.

If children are to gain the values inherent in open-ended materials, they need to have enough available so that they can carry out their ideas. They are likely to lose interest if they must wait too long to have access to the materials they wish to use. When there is a sufficient quantity, conflicts and frustrations can be avoided. A large sand area makes it possible for several children to play at the same time. Although each child does not need to have a pail, shovel and strainer, an adequate supply should be available so that play is not inhibited.

Programs should be planned so that children have enough time to play with the materials. There should be blocks of time available to explore and enjoy the pleasure of making their own discoveries. Individual children need time to practice newly developed skills at their own rate, in their own way, and to enjoy their mastery of these skills, thus gaining confidence in themselves as learners.

As children have opportunities to build on their newly developed skills, learning becomes exciting. For many days, Bruce cut triangular shapes of dough. Something about the shape seemed to intrigue him. One day he stacked them; another day he lined them up in a neat row; on yet another day he made a fancy border around the entire table. Then one day, with a look of surprise he shouted, "Look! I made a tree!"

Adult Intervention

The teacher or caregiver is central to the selection of materials, their placement in a classroom, and the arrangement of time and space for children to use them. A teacher's very presence shows support of a child's work. By making provisions for children to explore in their own unique ways, the teacher indicates acceptance of their individuality. Many caregivers and teachers are tempted to intervene in a child's explorations by showing the child a way of solving a problem, hoping to expedite learning. When this occurs, however, the child is denied the satisfaction of discovering problems and solving them for him or herself. As Piaget has said, ". . . children learn from trying to work out their own ways of doing things even if it does not end up as we might expect." According to Piaget, a teacher should study the ways a child solves problems by him or herself, and then provide suitable materials and media to assist the child as necessary (1973, pp. 24, 26).

When Aaron had difficulty making an entrance for cars to come into his parking lot, the teacher thought she knew a better way, but she refrained from

CHILDREN PLAY—CHILDREN LEARN

If a child is to develop competencies in reading, writing and mathematics, it is necessary to develop:

Visual memory
Auditory memory
Language acquisition
Classification
Hand-eye coordination
Body image
Spatial orientation

In order to develop these abilities, a child needs experiences with:

Configurations
Figure-ground relationships
Shapes
Patterns
Spatial relationships
Matching (shape, size, color)
Whole-part relationships

Arranging objects in sequence
Organizing objects in ascending
  and descending order
Classification
Verbal communication
Measurement
Solving problems

These concepts and skills can be acquired as a child has time and space to initiate activities with such open-ended materials as:

Blocks
Cubes
Pegs
Finger paint
Brush paint

Dough
Clay
Water
Sand
Wood

Thus, the basic concepts and skills for reading, writing and mathematics are learned as children . . .

PLAY

offering advice and gave Aaron time to do it himself. Annette was unable to find a way to make windows for her house. The teacher chose not to intervene and so there were no windows on her house. At a later date, Annette will have an opportunity to solve this problem for herself. If she had seemed frustrated by the problem, the teacher might have intervened by raising a question or making a suggestion. In this instance, neither was necessary.

Even open-ended materials can become "structured" materials if children are instructed in how to use them. While teachers have goals concerning children's use of materials and the learnings that can result, they should make it possible for individual children to set personal goals when they play with water, clay, blocks or paint. Teachers are concerned that children continue to develop and maintain a driving interest in learning, and that they acquire the skills they will need to be independent learners. As Ellis suggests, an appropriate environment "energizes the play behaviors" of children (1973, p. 79).

When teachers have carefully thought through the materials that will be made available and have planned a program that encourages children to play, they do not need to contrive activities intended to make learning fun—because children will have fun. They do not need to develop instructional exercises to facilitate children's learning because they learn as they play. What experience in matching size could have been better than the one Karen created for herself with dough as she placed all the large "cookies" in one row, the smaller ones in another row, and the tiny ones in the bottom row, and pointed to each row as she announced with glee, "Little, big, more bigger!"

References

Bruner, J., Jolla A., and Sylva, K., eds. *Play: Its Role in Development*. New York: Basic, 1976.

Christie, J., and Johnson, E.P. "The Role of Play in Social-Intellectual Development." *Review of Educational Research* 53, 1 (1983): 93-115.

Dewey, J. *Democracy and Education*. New York: Macmillan, 1916.

———. *Experience and Education*. New York: Macmillan, 1938.

Duckworth, E. "Piaget Takes a Teacher's Look." *Learning* 2 (1973): 22-27.

Ellis, M., Jr. *Why People Play*. Englewood Cliffs, NJ: Prentice Hall, 1973.

Hirsch, E., ed. *The Block Book*. Washington, DC: National Association for the Education of Young Children, 1973.

Lindberg, L., and Swedlow, R. *Early Childhood Education: A Guide for Observation and Participation* (2nd ed.). Boston: Allyn and Bacon, 1980.

Sutton-Smith, B., ed. *Play and Learning*. Somerset, NJ: Wiley, 1979.

Evaluating Children's Play Engagements for Social-Cognitive Growth

Judith A. Chafel and Mary Beth Childers

Judith A. Chafel is Associate Professor, Department of Curriculum and Instruction, Indiana University. Her research interests focus on the development of social cognition in young children.

Mary Beth Childers is an ED.S. Candidate in Instructional Systems Technology at Indiana University.

Social cognition refers to "the child's ability to think about his or her social world" (Rubin, 1980, p. 75). As Damon (1979) has pointed out, children's developing social conceptions of such "juicy topics" as friendship, leadership, popularity, rivalry and fairness are interesting enough in themselves to merit our attention. What does a consideration of topics such as these add to our understanding of child development? It yields insight into how children derive meaning from social encounters; categorize, order and interpret social reality; share ideas and perspectives with their peers; and influence and benefit from social experience (Damon, 1981). Additionally, the way in which children think about others has an important effect on how they behave with others. For example, a child who thinks a peer has deliberately destroyed his or her puzzle is likely to retaliate aggressively, whereas the interpretation that the destruction was accidental is less likely to result in physical abuse (Dodge, 1980; Shantz, 1983).

Children's "social-knowledge-in-action" (Shantz, 1983, p. 542) can be assessed naturalistically as they interact with others in routine, daily life activities. These activities will yield rich information because they are highly meaningful to children, and because children can freely construct their own social reality. Using the method of specimen description, an observer following the child "like a shadow" (Chan, 1978, p. 57) simply narrates sequentially "everything" that children say and do for a given period of time, along with a brief description of the immediate environmental context. Several references have

Acknowledgment: The authors would like to express appreciation to Jesse Goodman for his helpful comments during preparation of this work.

been devoted to this mode of observation (Almy and Genishi, 1979; Carew, Chan and Halfar, 1976; Cohen and Stern, 1978; Irwin and Bushnell, 1980; Wright, 1960). Irwin and Bushnell (1980, p. 100) define the goal of descriptive accounts as "picturing situations in words that are precise enough and complete enough that we, or anyone else, can use our records for later analysis." Observers should emphasize the description of behavior; interpretation comes only after the record is made. Wright (1960) provides a complete discussion of the technique, as well as a number of useful guidelines.

This article describes and interprets several vignettes, illustrating children's developing social conceptions related to three content areas of social cognition: children's knowledge of social rules, roles and settings. The specimen descriptions were collected as part of a research study, focusing on 4- and 5-year-old children in two preschool classrooms engaged at free play. Free play "represents a window to the child's mind"; because of this, we can infer the existence of cognitive competencies from observations of children at play (Rubin, Fein and Vandenberg, 1983, p. 756).

CHILDREN'S KNOWLEDGE OF SOCIAL RULES

A social rule may be defined as "the shared expectations about what should occur in face-to-face and co-acting social encounters" (Grimmett and Chafel, 1982, p. 55). Consider the following excerpt from a specimen record.

Two children are rolling cars along a race track.
P. says, "This is mine. I go first."
Y. replies, "Then me."
P. rolls the car down the track.
Y. adds, "Next me, P.," as he rolls his car.

The children were assigning roles for play by employing a sequencing strategy. The children's interactions were composed of turns at acting. A turn represented the contribution of one participant in the interchange (Garvey, 1974). Clearly, the children were demonstrating their understanding of rule-governed behavior: one could predict what would happen next in the play process. They were displaying evidence of their awareness of the fact that their social play depended upon mutually accepted "rules of the game."

Three children are messing about at the water table.
A. takes a baster from T.'s tub and gives it to C.
T. says excitedly, "Don't! A. took it away from me."
A. retorts, "Well, he didn't have any."
T. replies, "I had it first. I had it. I had it first!"
A. explains that C. didn't have any and needs to try it.
T. continues to argue, "I had it first. I get it!"

The children were expressing their ideas about what constitutes justice, or how to distribute play materials according to a system of mutually agreed upon rules. One child's rule was reflected by the comment "I had it first. I get it!," while another's was explained by the fact that "C. didn't have any and needs to try it." The children were confronting opposing points of view, as they

— Mary Beth Childers

articulated varying social conceptions about how to distribute property fairly, ownership and personal rights. They were "testing" their social knowledge in face-to-face interaction by arguing, and attempting to arrive at justification of a personal point of view. Both general procedural rules and rules for guiding behavior are essential to the conduct of social play (Garvey, 1974).

CHILDREN'S KNOWLEDGE OF SOCIAL ROLES

A social role may be defined as a system of "more or less integrated normative beliefs about how a person in that role should behave" (Grimmett and Chafel, 1982, p. 46). Consider this specimen description that illustrates the way in which children assign, accept and enact roles.

Three children are constructing with blocks.
H. queries, "What do we do with the wrench?"
R. directs, "Repair."
H. asks, "Screw it, right? Nail it, right?"
R. explains, "I'm using a hammer. You're using a hammer and he's using a hammer, okay? Get it done."
H. queries, "You tell us what to do."
R. replies, "You do big, me small."

Social roles consist of socially shared expectations; they refer to relationships between two or more persons. In the example, the children were revealing their ideas about what leaders and followers do. Structuring their play to accommodate the two complementary positions, they were voluntarily accepting the assigned role differentiations, and coordinating their behavior with one another according to a mutually agreed upon plan.

Two children are building with interlocking toys.
R. remarks, "I'm an American. Who are you? Want to be my friend?"
P. replies, "Yes."
R. continues, "Okay, but you help me make a fort, okay? Make a house, okay?"
P. agrees, "Okay. I have an Indian and a bow and arrow."

Play provides a means of initiating a friendship. The children were interacting as friends, and their actions yield insight into how they comprehended the friendship relation. Their actions displayed their knowledge that friends do the same pleasurable activities: they play together, they do things for one another and they share play objects. The children understood the rules by which peers interact as friends in a concrete, practical way.

CHILDREN'S KNOWLEDGE OF SOCIAL SETTINGS

A social setting may be defined as "a context or 'situation' in which social encounters occur" (Grimmett and Chafel, 1982, p. 63). Settings represent situational influences on children's social exchanges. Consider this narrative account.

O. has been playing at the housekeeping area. K. walks over carrying a piece
of art work she has just completed. K. proudly shows off her work.

K. says, "Mom! Look what I did!"

O. responds maternally, "Good! Go put it up where the others are, okay?"

K. goes off to do what she's been told.

The children were manifesting an awareness that certain activities occur in particular places. In this instance, the children reflected their knowledge that a dramatic play area in preschool prescribes the following message: "This is fantasy!" One child in the example assumed the pretend role of mother, while another took on the role of child. These behaviors were supported by the shared expectations of the children concerning reasons for gathering in this social setting, as well as the physical objects and arrangements in that setting. Because of the setting's prescribed messages, the children quickly entered into a dramatic play mode.

Two children are dressing up at the dramatic play area.

O. announces, "We be pretty tonight." "We go to a wedding tonight, okay?"
"You need something to wear to the wedding."

N. exclaims, "I wear this because it's cold." N. puts a shawl around her shoulders.

O. comments, "Very nice!"

The children were using the "as-if" context of fantasy play to communicate their understandings of social reality. They appreciated the fact that a wedding, as a very special social occasion, required "dress-up" clothes, as exemplified by one child's statement, "We be pretty tonight." "We go to a wedding tonight, okay?" An analysis of children's exchanges at play can tell us much about their conceptions of the social world. "As we gain more skill and experience, we know better how to look at children, what to look for, and how to interpret what we see" (Phinney, 1982, p. 24).

DRAWING IMPLICATIONS FOR TEACHERS

Taking the time to observe and assess children's play engagements is important. Educators need to develop a comprehensive understanding of children, thereby gaining valuable insight into how to guide their social-cognitive growth. Naturalistic observation is an effective and useful method of assessing the social skills and deficiencies of individual children. Utilizing this method in the classroom requires preparation, objective observation skills and the ability to draw accurate interpretations.

Preparation for Observing Children's Play

Allocating time to observe children's play and sensitizing ourselves to the various aspects of social behavior are two important prerequisites to assessing a child's social-cognitive growth through naturalistic observations. While the idea of setting aside adequate time to observe is a simplistic one, it is frequently overlooked due to the daily demands of teaching. Therefore, it is important to reserve and integrate a period of observation time into a daily schedule. Of equal importance is the need to sensitize ourselves to the various aspects of a child's social behavior. An effort should be made to look at the world through a child's eyes, so that observations are not out of context but reflect the child's perspective. For example, in the vignette illustrating friendship, an observer who is not sensitive to the dynamics of the children's social behavior might interpret this interplay as a show of manipulation. Someone sensitized to children's play behaviors, however, would identify R.'s need for approval from his playmate.

Observation Techniques

The validity and usefulness of an observation are greatly enhanced when the observer strives to be objective and unobtrusive. Objectivity is necessary in order to gain an authentic picture of the child's social behaviors. Assume, for example, that an observer is taking a specimen record, recording descriptions of verbal exchanges, physical actions and facial expressions as they occur. In order to obtain a realistic view of the child's social skills and needs, recording these events precisely is important, avoiding vague and judgmental descriptions that may reflect some bias or distortion. A careful observer must also be unobtrusive. If children are overtly aware that they are the focal point of an observation, they are likely to alter their behavior, resulting in an observation that is no longer representative of their usual behavior. Moving into an area slowly, avoiding eye contact with the children, and placing yourself in the area where you are not readily noticeable will assist efforts at being unobtrusive.

Interpreting the Observations

Based on objective observations, an observer can then make interpretations about the kinds of social competencies discussed in this article: taking turns for play, justice concerning the use of play materials, understanding what leaders and followers do, friendship, appropriate behavior for a play setting, and dress for a social occasion. We can infer, for example, from a child who asks permission before entering into a play activity that the child has developed the social awareness of peer acceptance and cooperation. Likewise, we can infer from a child who abruptly demands entry into play activities by taking another child's play possessions that this child lacks the social skills needed for acceptance and cooperative play. Having identified aspects of a child's social cognition which are deficient, we can then offer appropriate guidance. Through careful observation and interpretation of children's play engagements, we can gain valuable insight into the social competencies and needs of the children we teach.

As a final point, we emphasize that the vignettes described in this article do not represent merely "kid stuff." On the contrary, *they reflect children's serious attempts to construct meaningful social concepts.* Teachers and parents need to respect this constructive process, enabling children to become reflective about their social-cognitive knowledge.

Children's Books

Barkin, C., and James, E. *Are We Still Best Friends?* Milwaukee, WI: Raintree, 1975.

Bonsall, C. *It's Mine.* New York: Harper, 1964.

Charlip, R., and Supree, B. *Harlequin and the Gift of Many Colors.* New York: Parent's Magazine Press, 1973.

Minarik, E.H. *No Fighting, No Biting.* New York: Harper, 1958.

Robinson, N. *Veronica the Show-Off.* New York: Four Winds, 1982.

Sharmat, M. *I'm Not Oscar's Friend Anymore.* New York: Dutton, 1975.

Sherman, I. *I Do Not Like It when My Friend Comes To Visit.* San Diego, CA: Harcourt, 1975.

Simon, N. *I Was So Mad.* Niles, IL: Whitman, 1974.

Slobodkin, L. *Excuse Me; Certainly.* New York: Vanguard, 1959.

Udry, J. *Let's Be Enemies.* New York: Harper, 1961.

Warburg, S. *I Like You.* New York: Houghton, 1965.

Zolotow, C. *The Hating Book.* New York: Harper, 1969.

_____. *The Quarreling Book.* New York: Harper, 1963.

Books for Teachers

Almy, M., and Genishi, C. *Ways of Studying Children.* New York: Teachers College Press, 1979.

Boehm, A. *The Classroom Observer: A Guide for Developing Observation Skills.* New York: Teachers College Press, 1977.

Carew, J., Chan, I., and Halfar, C. *Observing Intelligence in Young Children: Eight Case Studies.* Englewood Cliffs, NJ: Prentice-Hall, 1976.

Chan, I. "Observing Young Children, a Science; Working with Them, an Art." *Young Children* 33 (1978): 54-63.

Cohen, D., and Stern, V. *Observing and Recording the Behavior of Young Children.* New York: Teachers College Press, 1978.

Medinnus, G. *Child Study and Observation Guide.* New York: Wiley, 1976.

Phinney, J. "Observing Children: Ideas for Teachers." *Young Children* 37 (1982): 16-24.

Rowan, B. *The Children We See: An Observational Approach to Child Study.* New York: Holt, 1973.

Books For Teacher Educators

Damon, W. "Why Study Social-Cognitive Development?" *Human Development* 22 (1979): 206-11.

_____. "Exploring Children's Social Cognition on Two Fronts." In J. Flavell and L. Ross, eds., *Social Cognitive Development: Frontiers and Possible Futures.* Cambridge: Cambridge University Press, 1981.

Dodge, K.A. "Social Cognition and Children's Aggressive Behavior." *Child Development* 51 (1980): 162-70.

Garvey, C. "Some Properties of Social Play." *Merrill-Palmer Quarterly* 20 (1974): 163-80.

Grimmett, S., and Chafel, J. *Cognition of Social Organization: Underlying Competence and Its Measurement.* Tech. Rep. on HHS/ACYF No. 105-81-C-008. Tucson: University of Arizona, 1982.

Irwin, D., and Bushnell, M. *Observational Strategies for Child Study.* New York: Holt, 1980.

Rubin, K. "Fantasy Play: Its Role in the Development of Social Skills and Cognition." In K. Rubin, ed., *Children's Play.* San Francisco: Jossey-Bass, 1980.

Rubin, K., Fein, G., and Vandenberg, B. "Play." In E. Mavis Hetherington, ed., *Handbook of Child Psychology,* Vol. 4: *Socialization, Personality and Social Development.* New York: Wiley, 1983.

Shantz, C. "Social Cognition." In J. Flavell and E. Markham, eds., *Handbook of Child Psychology,* Vol. 3: *Cognitive Development.* New York: Wiley, 1983.

Touliatos, J., and Compton, H. *Approaches to Child Study.* Minneapolis: Burgess, 1983.

Wright, H. "Observational Child Study." In P. Mussen, ed., *Handbook of Research in Child Development.* New York: Wiley, 1960.

_____. *Recording and Analyzing Child Behavior.* New York: Harper, 1967.

The Role of the Teacher in Children's Play

Sharon Elliott

Sharon Elliott is Director, Wayne State University Nursery School at Jeffries Homes. She is past President of Michigan Association for the Education of Young Children and active in child advocacy.

"If the rule structure of human play and games sensitizes the child to the rules of culture, both generally and in preparation for a particular way of life, then surely play must have some special role in nurturing symbolic activity in general. For culture is symbolism in action" (Bruner, 1976, p. 19). If play has a special role in nurturing symbolic activity, then the teacher who is working with the young child must have a special role in furthering this play activity and thus in furthering symbolic activity and culture.

A basic activity period during the preschool day is self-selection/self-direction or play time. A casual observer may have difficulty seeing the organization, the planning and the evaluation that have taken place in order for this time to be productive, fun and educational. One enters the classroom and sees two children painting at the paint easels. A paraprofessional talks with them as they work. Across the room are four children in the block area dressed in white caps and smocks speculating about x-rays, fixing the baby and giving shots. Still others are in the dress-up/kitchen area complete with hats, purses, bags, talking about eating breakfast and then going to church. In the center of the room at a low table sit four children working puzzles and laughing with the teacher. One child is in the language arts area looking at a book. Another is typing. And to complete the picture, one child sits sucking his thumb and looking out the window.

Are the children simply "playing" on the basis of their own interests? Or is this a picture of a highly structured (organized) room where things are going according to plan? Indeed, this is the well-planned classroom. Children have been to a hospital and are making plans to visit a church. Their play is both a presentation of what has been and anticipation of what is to come. The other activities described reflect the teacher's awareness of the need for adult-child communication that furthers language skills and of children's need for small muscle and hand-eye coordination projects, their need for expression of creative abilities while experimenting with the properties of paint, and their need for time for reflection and privacy.

The Teacher's Roles

In this classroom the teacher (1) *sustains the play,* (2) *modifies the play* and (3) *extends the play.* She sustains the play as she moves to each of the different room areas for a few minutes, observing, smiling, commenting and giving recognition to what the children are doing. She modifies the play when she helps children reach a decision about what they would rather do, play church with the others or work the puzzles, but suggests that taking puzzles to the housekeeping area may create too much confusion. She extends the play when she offers additional props such as a stethoscope and bandages, raises questions and makes suggestions. Hendrick (1980) describes the teacher who is skilled in generating creative play as one who sees play from the child's point of view and "casts herself in the role of supportive assistant to the child . . . she thinks constantly of what she might offer to sustain or extend . . . the play" (p. 196).

In addition to the three roles described above, the teacher must also (4) *evaluate the play* and (5) *interpret it to others.* Today's early childhood teachers find themselves in the position of having to defend play time for children to administrators and to parents. If they cannot, it soon becomes a 15-minute period sandwiched between formal mathematics readiness, language arts readiness and social studies periods. Worse than that, play time may be removed completely with the edict "We can't afford to have our children play; they must learn the academics."

Teachers must understand what play is and is not before they can interpret it to others. The effective teacher keeps a few, cogent anecdotal notes during play time. He or she watches a child for 5-10 minutes, recording what the child says and does and what is said and done to the child during that period of time. Once a number of these vignettes have been recorded, the teacher uses them to study activities the child chooses over a period of time and to examine the following: Is there a balance of activities or does the child consistently choose the same activity? Are other children involved? What is the quality of those interactions? What level of communication skills does the child demonstrate? What kind of problem-solving occurs during the play? What understanding and lack of understanding does the child demonstrate? Are there examples of classification, grouping, seriation? This naturalistic information can be shared in a parent conference or compiled and used as general information in newsletters to parents. It can also be used with administrators and other staff to help them understand how children learn through play.

Educational/Non-Educational Play

Spodek (1978) makes a distinction between educational and non-educational play, stating that ". . . educational play has as its prime purpose the child's learning" (p. 239). It is enjoyed by the child, it is personally satisfying, but its primary purpose is learning. He describes four types of educational play usually found in nursery school and kindergarten classes: manipulative, physical, dramatic play and games with rules.

With *manipulative play* the adult should carefully select materials that ensure a degree of difference in complexity so as to engage the capabilities of all the children in the class. Manipulatives should be accessible and inviting to the children. They include puzzles, small building toys such as Legos, objects that can be put together and taken apart. The teacher displays these materials on low open shelves in one section of the room. During self-selection time children are free to select these materials. As they play the teacher observes the coordination displayed, persistence to the task chosen and the imagination involved in creating the structures.

Physical play often includes that part of the day called "outdoor time." At this time children have the opportunity to use large muscles, to run, to climb and to tumble. It is seldom that teachers have the luxury of helping to design a playground. An effective teacher, however, can study the existing facility and supplement what is available. If the playground is a traditional one with swings and slides, the teacher can add wheel toys and make available water, sand and loose parts such as tires, crates and boards for building. The teacher can purchase hoops, make can stilts and save large boxes for dramatic play. The teacher's role outside is the same as inside: to sustain the play, modify the play and extend the play.

One of the best teaching strategies for learning in nursery school and kindergarten is the use of *dramatic play*. Smith, Goodman and Meredith (1970) discuss education as a "coming to know through the symbolic transformation of experience" (p. 74). This educational process (based on a free elaboration of Suzanne Langer's formulations) involves three stages of mental activity:

1. Perceiving new data in the environment. Perceiving includes meeting a new object, happening or idea.
2. Ideating upon the perceptions. Ideating includes conceptualizing and generalizing, coming to terms with an object, happening or idea.
3. Presenting ideations to oneself and others.

These stages hold true for young children engaged in dramatic play. When playing they may be either at level two or level three. At one time they are playing with an idea. At another time they are presenting their understandings.

A simple way to build a quality dramatic play component is the establishment of prop boxes that store the materials for a particular role (x-ray technician, dentist, office worker, librarian, ballet dancer, mechanic, painter and airline pilot). These boxes include something for the child to wear, like a hat or tools, something that suggests "I am a . . . . " The prop box also provides an opportunity for the teacher to collect supplemental materials over a period of time (i.e., hospital smock, stethoscope, tongue depressors, gauze bandages, x-rays).

Children coming to the block area during self-selection time see a display that invites them to begin playing. The smock and stethoscope are draped over several blocks arranged to look like a bed on which a doll is lying. This type of stimulation invites the child to enter the area and to begin to play. The teacher does not assign children to the area, designating one to be the doctor and one to be the patient. Those who are interested come over and are left to their own devices; there may be five doctors and one patient. As they play the teacher may see a need for other materials and thus in an unobtrusive way extend the play. As he or she watches, the teacher notes the vocabulary used by the child. Does the child understand and use the terms central to the theme of the play? Can the child enter into the play? Understand the selected role? Unobtrusively sustain the role effectively enough to engage the other children? Exit as necessary?

In dramatic play the teacher is often called upon to modify the play because of the need to help one child enter the play who wasn't initially involved. The teacher may have to suggest a role. For example, in playing house children will suggest that a less capable child play the role of the baby. Because that role may be seen as "babyish," some children are unwilling to accept the role. The teacher can suggest an alternative role such as aunt, uncle, babysitter—one that is agreeable to all. The teacher now has the child accepted in the play and can work to help him or her develop the social skills needed to remain in the group.

Children's presentations in dramatic play are a reflection of both what they understand and what they are confused about. This information serves as data for curriculum planning. For example, one group of preschool children expressed an interest in playing firefighter and asked for the firefighter prop box. The children pulled out hats, boots and pieces of hose. The teacher observed for about five minutes. Suddenly she realized that several children in the group thought firefighters made the fire. She had to decide whether to step in immediately and attempt to clarify their misunderstandings by asking questions and providing specific information or mentally file it for later discussion, introduction of books and stories, and a possible field trip.

Many teachers are ambivalent about entering children's play; not all teachers are comfortable with this role. A teacher may feel a need to enter the play in order to sustain it, refocus some children and extend the level of experimentation. The teacher, however, must be careful not to dominate the play or to stay too long in the play. Otherwise, there is the danger that children may begin playing for the teacher rather than with each other and the unique benefits of play may be lost.

Teachers make note of the use of props. In the firefighter play, some children may be very upset if they do not have an opportunity to use the hose. Others can work on a more symbolic level and let a block or their finger stand for the hose. Children are thrilled with props and will incorporate them easily into their play. Props can increase the richness of the play. They may, however, also limit the direction the play takes. Because children are at different developmental stages, props are used in different ways. For some children they become the main focus; they are actually more interested in playing with the props and exploring their properties. For others the props are a means to an end; the pretend play is the most important factor in the situation.

Children in preschool and kindergarten are beginning to enjoy *games with rules* but the teacher must be careful that this type of activity does not occupy a disproportionate period of time. Children may choose to play simple board games that reinforce counting, matching, knowledge of colors, numerals and letters (such as Candyland, Uno or Memory). They also enjoy simple chase and ball games such as Duck, Duck, Goose. In the initial stage they are taught the rules of the game. The teacher plays with the children to keep the game going and to help them thoroughly understand the game. Occasionally, one child wants to modify the rules and is able to convince others to accept his or her changes. This may be upsetting, however, to some who are insistent upon playing exactly according to the rules. The effective teacher assures children that if they agree it is all right to deviate from the rules and play the new way, but that they do not have to.

Helping the Non-Playing Child

In every classroom there are children who do not play, who do not wear the role of student very well. These children may come from distressed families and may be either aggressive or passive. They often hit, scratch, fight or sit withdrawn, speaking reluctantly when spoken to. Wolfgang (1977) sees these children at one end of a continuum that seeks internalization of impulse control and, through intervention, hopes to move them to a point where they can adapt and ". . . maintain expressive control over their actions with objects and others . . . ." (p. 8).

In order to help these children, Wolfgang provides a model of intervention that is also a continuum moving from directive to nondirective intervention (p. 21):

Basic Teacher Behavior Continuum

Directive ――――――――――――――――――――――――――――― Nondirective

(1) Physical   (2) Verbal   (4) Nondirective
     help or   directions   statements
     modeling

                         (3) Verbal   (5) Visual
                            questions   looking on

Every program has such children. In helping an aggressive child learn to play in a more productive way, the effective teacher prevents the child from being labeled as a "bad child" by other children in the class. Through this intervention, the passive child is saved from being overlooked by others in the group and from feelings of isolation.

Summary

Play is natural to most children. It involves a concern with the process rather than the end product. Play is initiated and ended at the discretion of the child. It affords children an opportunity to work through problems. In describing the educational implications of Piaget's views on play, Day and Parker (1977) say that ". . . Children should be encouraged to use their initiative and intelligence in actively manipulating the environment because it is only by dealing directly with reality that the basic biological capacity for intelligence develops. Children's spontaneous play should be the primary context in which teachers encourage the use of intelligence and initiative" (p. 372). Thus, it is a knowledgeable, creative and talented teacher who structures the classroom and his or her own roles to enable children to take advantage of learning through play.

References

Bruner, J.S., Jolly, A., and Sylva, K. Play—Its Role in Development and Education. New York: Basic Books, 1976.

Day, M.C., and Parker, R.K. The Preschool in Action: Exploring Early Childhood Programs. Boston: Allyn and Bacon, 1977.

Hendrick, J. The Whole Child: New Trends in Early Education. St. Louis: Mosby, 1980.

Smith, E.B., Goodman, K.S., and Meredith, R. Language and Thinking in the Elementary School. New York: Holt, 1970.

Spodek, B. Teaching in the Early Years (2nd ed.). Englewood Cliffs, NJ: Prentice-Hall, 1978.

Wolfgang, C.H. Helping Aggressive and Passive Preschoolers Through Play. Columbus, OH: Merrill, 1977.

Play Materials and Activities for Children Birth to 10 Years:

People, Play, Props and Purposeful Development

Judy Spitler McKee

Judy Spitler McKee is Professor of Early Childhood Education and Educational Psychology, Eastern Michigan University. Her publications and areas of specialization are on applications of Piagetian research, play, and helping young children in crisis situations.

> We never educate directly, but indirectly by
> means of the environment.   *John Dewey*
>
> Through play, children learn what no one can
> teach them.   *Lawrence K. Frank*

One of the most critical and complex decisions with which caregivers and teachers must struggle is how to arrange and rearrange play environments that will maximize young children's growth, development and learning and capitalize on individual interests and aptitudes. Equipping an early childhood program or a playroom requires, in addition to money and time, professional planning, monitoring and evaluating. Many factors must be considered in selecting materials and activities: the developmental ages and stages of the children being served; their individual health or handicaps; safety features and supervision requirements; embedded values (humane, culturally accurate, non-racist, non-sexist); learning possibilities; purposes of the program (educational, developmental or therapeutic); and the quality of fun-ness, which sparks players and produces persistence of playing.

Planning for and evaluating safety aspects necessitate that certain materials and activities only be used with adult supervision, particularly with very young, handicapped, abused or distressed children. As adults knowledgeably intervene by modeling play and playfulness and monitoring children's play, they need to be vigilant not to interfere or take control from the children—or play stops. Adults who observe children's different play actions, reactions and interactions will gather invaluable information about developmental levels, styles of learning and problem areas that are not apparent in adult-directed, work-based situations. Objective information about children's attitudes, abilities, skills, concepts, interests and stressors obtained during play observations can then be reported to parents and professionals. When personal, helpful information is communicated about the special developmental, educational and therapeutic benefits of play materials and activities for young children, parents often enthusiastically support educators' efforts and supply free materials from home or business.

The following tables represent a range of possibilities for varied play materials and activities that could be provided for pleasurable and profitable engagements for children from birth to 10 years. Only a few, carefully selected materials and activities should be provided at one time since too many are overwhelming and change children's play. As educators observe, monitor and evaluate children at play, they will make changes in the play environments, adding and deleting materials and modifying activities to create closer matches among people, play and props to ensure developmental progress.

Four developmental stages are represented: The Infant Stage (birth to 1½ years), The Toddler Stage (1½ to 3 years), The Play Stage (3 to 7 years) and The Work Stage (7 to 10 years). Due to wide variations in individual development, the concept of "stage" refers less to chronological age (C.A. or birthday age) and more to what psychologists term "developmental age," which represents a way of expressing how the whole child is functioning.

The areas included are: (1) Gross Motor, (2) Fine Motor, (3) Construction, (4) Adult Partner Games, (5) Social-Emotional, (6) Make-Believe, (7) Activity Areas, (8) Language and (9) Travel.

Travel

While art materials and books are attention-holders for young children, very few have been included as travel suggestions because they require close concentration that may be too visually taxing in a moving vehicle and contribute to motion-sickness. A deep cake pan, or a cookie sheet, can be modified for travel purposes. Sponge or felt can be glued to the bottom so felt figures can adhere more readily and will not be lost. For children of all ages, taking along a "security" blanket, special pillow or favorite stuffed animal is helpful.

➡

References

Dewey, J. *Democracy and Education*. New York: Macmillan, 1961 (original publication 1916).

Frank, L.K. "Play and Child Development." Reprinted in P. Markun, ed., *Play: Children's Business*. Wheaton, MD: Association for Childhood Education International, 1974.

See also:

Allen, A., and Neterer, E. "A Guide to Play Materials." In P. Markun, ed., *Play: Children's Business*. Wheaton, MD: Association for Childhood Education International, 1974.

Sutton-Smith, B., and Sutton-Smith, S. *How To Play with Your Children*. New York: Hawthorne, 1974.

The Infant Stage: Birth to 1½ Years

GROSS MOTOR

Rocker
Cradle gym
Beanbag chair
Infant bouncers
Pillows for positioning
Wooden bar across crib or buggy to
    hit and kick dangling objects
Brightly colored balls

FINE MOTOR

Rattles
Colorful mobiles
Colored stacking rings
Grip ball
Busy board with knobs, doors, clear
    pictures
Plastic colored keys or animals on
    hoop

Teething rings
Three-piece homemade puzzle from
    cereal box
Large pop beads
Floating bath toys

CONSTRUCTION

Cardboard boxes to stack and knock
    down
Cardboard blocks
Homemade carton blocks covered
    with colorful contact paper or
    fabric
Plastic containers to fill and dump
Buckets, baskets, shovels
Large and medium-size plastic or
    rubber balls

Illustrations by Sheila McKee-Lee

ADULT PARTNER GAMES

EARLY in Period:
Sing to baby
Name special people for baby:
  Mommy, Miss Carol
Wave "bye-bye" to baby
Imitate baby's speech
Ask "Where's baby?" in front of
  mirror
Play "Peek-a-Boo" with person or
  object
Play "Pat-a-Cake," "This Little
  Piggy," "How Big Is Baby?"

LATER in Period:
Name body parts; ask "Where's your
  nose?"
Use cloth hand puppet
Play "Hear-a-Boo" with hidden
  sounds
Read simple books with exaggerated
  expression
Play book "Peek-a-Boo"
Play "1-2-3, Upsey, Daisey!"
Roll ball with baby; have baby
  retrieve ball
Use large pop beads with baby

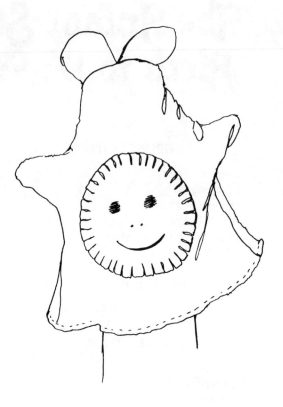

SOCIAL-EMOTIONAL

Soft blanket or pillow
Cuddly, stuffed one-piece animal or
  doll with no ingestable parts
Homemade smiling face or sun hand
  puppet; friendly face paper plate
  puppet
Social games of "Peek-a-Boo," "Pat-
  a-Cake" and books or toys with
  this theme
Homemade "Peek-a-Boo" window
  book with family pictures
Large photographs of family or
  childcare staff
Pictures of babies
Cassette tape of lullabies
Cassette tape of voices of family
  members or caregivers

MAKE-BELIEVE

Stuffed animals, especially
  storybook characters
One-piece baby doll
Bounce-back, weighted doll (roly-
  poly toy)
Realistic dolls, vehicles and
  furniture with no removable parts
Cloth and stiff cardboard books with
  simple, clear pictures

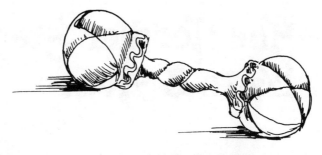

ACTIVITY AREAS

Fun-To-Hold Area
(Grasping Skills)

Stuffed one-piece animal
Multi-textured ball, quilt, octopus, gloves: corduroy, satin, lace, sheepskin, terrycloth
Grip (clutch) balls
Several types of rattles
Hoop with dangling objects
Graduated stacking rings
Soft balls and blocks
Cardboard or homemade carton blocks
Large wooden spoons
Pots and pans and large lids
Baby drinking cup, plastic dishes, bowls
Cloth books; thick cardboard books
Nesting or stacking cups or cubes (remove smallest ones)
Three-piece "cereal" puzzle mounted on thick cardboard

Fun-To-Hear Area
(Auditory Skills)

Sound-makers: rattles, balls with embedded bells or squeakers
Cage toy with bell inside
Squeak toys: clothespin, animals, dolls, blocks
Clear containers with screw-on lids with colored balls inside: ping pong, plastic or fish bobbers minus wires
Sound canisters with buttons, pebbles, marbles, small rubber ball, cotton
Wind chimes and bells
Simple jack-in-the-box
Simple music box
Simple music instruments: maracas, wrist bells, bells on handles
Doll that cries or says "Mama"
Cassette of soothing or dance music

LANGUAGE

Family photograph album
Objects with motion that stimulate speech: stacking rings, balls
Realistic one- or two-piece cars, trucks, boats, buses
Bells securely sewn to booties or wrist bands or on cloth puppet
Safe mirror rattle
Cassette of nursery rhymes or animal sounds
Adult coverall apron with many pockets for familiar objects
Reading books: nursery rhymes, *Pat the Bunny, Goodnight Moon, Babies, The Pudgy Peek-a-Boo Book, Teddy Bear's Day*

TRAVEL

Terrycloth hand puppet
Plastic hoop with dangling objects
Suction toy
Diaper or towel for "Peek-a-Boo" play
"Peek-a-Boo" dolly
Soft teether
Unbreakable mirror
Cloth grip animal or ball
Washable cloth book
Stiff cardboard book with clear pictures
Small family photograph album
Small album with magazine pictures of babies and families
Cassette of lullabies or soothing music (Halpern)

The Toddler Stage: 1½ to 3 Years

GROSS MOTOR

Safe, simple climber with wooden
stairs and slide
Crawl-through tunnel
Rocking chair
Rocking boat
Baby buggy
Riders: trucks, cars
Oversized cardboard boxes to crawl
through, sit in
Push-and-pull toys: lawn mower,
popcorn popper, clacking animals
Big balls to toss and chase
Beanbag chair

CONSTRUCTION

Sand play equipment: pails, shovels,
scoops, containers, colanders,
large gelatin molds
Large soft blocks
Homemade carton blocks covered
with paper or fabric
Large wooden blocks
Stacking or nesting materials: cubes,
eggs, cans
Milk-bottle carriers and crates
Plastic laundry baskets

FINE MOTOR

Push-down, pop-up materials
Soft foam and rubber balls
Wooden vehicles
Wooden train set
Stacking or nesting materials: cubes,
eggs, cans (remove smallest one)
Canister with clip and wooden
clothespins
Dressing dolls, pillows or books
with velcro shapes, large snaps,
zippers, buttons
Simple wooden puzzles with knobs,
3-D and block puzzles
Pounding board
Slinky
Bells on handles, wrist bells,
maracas, tambourine
Color paddles

ADULT PARTNER GAMES

Play "Ashes, Ashes" and "Pop Goes
the Weasel"
Play simple "Hide-and-Seek" with
persons and objects
Play "Fill-and-Dump": wrap up
child's favorite play item; let child
unwrap it
"Fill-and-Dump" race: put items in
containers very fast; let toddler
take them out
Recite and read nursery rhymes with
child
Play "Guess What's in the Pocket"
with pocket-style apron
Model prosocial puppet play for
child
Play reversal of power games:
"Who's the Boss?"

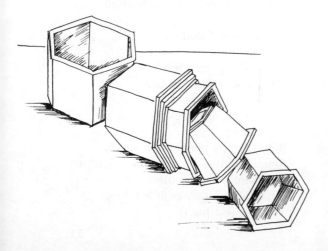

SOCIAL-EMOTIONAL

Dolls, boy and girl, differing ethnic
  groups
Doll buggy and medium-size doll
  house furniture
Realistic rubber or wooden animals
Friendly animal and person hand
  puppets

Tubbable doll
Bath toys
Pots and pans with lids
Two play telephones
Adult multi-pocket apron for
  "surprises"

MAKE-BELIEVE

Dolls and doll furniture
Miniature dishes, tea set and kettle
Miniature vehicles: cars, trucks,
  buses, boats
Stuffed animals
Dress-up clothes: plastic sunglasses,
  hats, pocketbooks, wallets, shoes
Nursery rhyme books and cassette
  tapes of storybooks
Movement and exercise records

ACTIVITY AREAS

Suggestions: Cover sand or water table containers with plastic tablecloth and weight the corners. Protect floors with plastic runners, provide coverups and extra dry clothing. Store extra props in boxes. Set and maintain firm limits on keeping water and sand in specified area. No-throwing and no-running rules need to be modeled by adults. Put colored tape on floor around area to delineate sand and water areas for children.

Sand

Buckets
Shovels, scoops, serving spoons
Plastic containers for filling and
  dumping

Water

Pails and pitchers
Containers of differing sizes
Colanders, strainers, funnels
Measuring cups and spoons

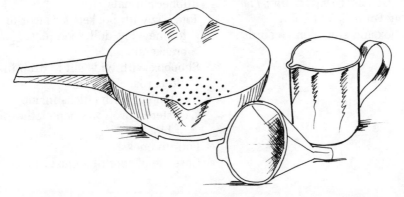

(Sand)

Gelatin molds
Muffin, pie and cake pans
Cookie cutters
Spoons, forks, spatulas
Sock with holes in toe
Rollers and dowels
Different size sifters, strainers,
    funnels
Miniature vehicles to bury
Dump truck and rocks
Magnifying glass

(Water)

Small watering can
Squeeze and spray bottles
Basters
Sponges
Rotary egg beaters
Boats
"Floaters" and "sinkers": corks,
    spools, seashells, utensils, wood
Diluted food coloring
Mild liquid soap
Soap-bubble pipes (no wires)
Dolls and dishes to wash
Pail of pebbles and rocks

LANGUAGE

Wooden play family
Wooden vehicles
Stuffed animals
Toy telephones
Farm and wild animal sets
Push-and-pull toys
Human doll to wash, dress or put to
    bed
Dress-up hats, belts, shoes, mirror
Feel bag or sock: balls, cotton, wood,
    silverware
"Peek-a-Boo" books and dolls
Reading books: nursery rhymes,
    pop-up books, action-oriented
    themes (*Hop on Pop; One Fish Two
    Fish Red Fish Blue Fish;
    Berenstains' B Book; Fox in Socks;
    Goodnight Moon; The Three
    Bears; Mr. Brown Can Moo! Can
    You?; Gobble, Growl, Grunt; The
    Pudgy Pat-a-Cake Book*)
Music box and sing-along records

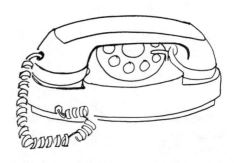

TRAVEL

Draw a face on child's palm and
    fingers with felt marker for puppet
Draw face on cloth and tie to child's
    hand for puppet
Small cloth doll
Rubber animals
Tote bag with pockets for favorite
    toy, new toy, doll, food (e.g.,
    crackers)
Shoebox with wide slit to drop in
    old cards
Knitted egg with chicks inside
Canister to drop wooden clothespins
    or blocks
Pop-up books
Cassette of soothing music

The Play Stage: 3 to 7 Years

GROSS MOTOR

Jungle gym
Safe swing
Indoor climber
Old tire and tunnel for obstacle
   course
Large riding animals on wheels
Wagon or wheelbarrow
Easy-to-straddle-and-pedal 3-
   wheeled vehicles
Beanbags and large wastebasket or
   bucket

CONSTRUCTION

Wooden, hollow and unit blocks
Wheelbarrow or wagon
Boards for building and hauling
Cardboard, foam and plastic shape
   blocks
Interlocking blocks: Large Legos,
   Bristle, rings
Large Tinker Toys and Lincoln Logs
Construct-o-Straws
Miniature wooden people
Miniature vehicles, both realistic
   and free-form types
Sand table and equipment

FINE MOTOR

Metal nuts and bolts
Small garden tools
Barrel of Monkeys: large and small
   types
Slinky
Beanbags of differing sizes and
   shapes
Blunt-end, wooden pick-up sticks
Large beads to string
Cookie cutters
Puzzles of graduated difficulty:
   whole object puzzles, simple
   puzzles with knobs, 10-50 piece
   puzzles of favorite characters
Picture Lotto
Wooden lacing/tying shoe
Parquetry blocks and pattern cards
Simple stamp pad
Simple printing set

ADULT PARTNER GAMES

EARLY in Period:
Play house with child
Build with child
Cut and paste with child
Carry on pretend and real telephone
   conversations
Pantomime animals
Read cartoons to child
Act out favorite stories
Use topsy-turvey talk

LATER in Period:
Model prosocial puppet play
Invent stories and situations
Invent songs and movements
Tell stories with child in dialogue
   form: "Your turn. And then . . ."
Play "What if" stories

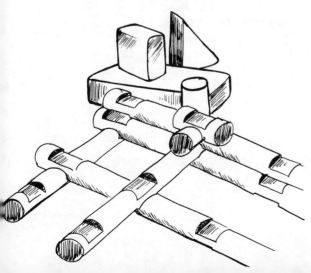

SOCIAL-EMOTIONAL

Stuffed animals
Oversized stuffed animals to
    "operate" on
Baby and preteen dolls
Soft-sculpture boy and girl dolls
Easy-on-and-off doll clothes
Large doll to wash
Playhouse area: stove, sink,
    refrigerator, table, chairs
"Mr. Rogers" and "Sesame Street"
    puppets and dolls
Family and animal puppets
Punching, weighted clown that
    bounces back

Water table and equipment
Soap-bubble pipes
Finger painting
Beanbags to throw
Adult multi-pocket apron for
    familiar objects and "surprises"
Soothing music for nap or rest

MAKE-BELIEVE

Blanket over chairs or table for
    "tent" or "hidden place"
Dishes and dishpan
Tea set and kettle
Picnic basket
Dress-up clothes: hats, jewelry,
    shoes, belts
Storybook puppets and character
    masks
Homemade stand-up paper figures:
    persons or animals
Fantasy storybooks and records
Two telephones
Medical kit
Viewmaster
Play money
Miniature or real camping items:
    knapsack, canteen

ACTIVITY AREAS

Play Dough
(To Make and Use)

Use on wooden or masonite boards;
    store in airtight containers or
    plastic bags; flour, salt, water,
    cooking oil
Picture (rebus) recipe
Rollers or dowels
Sturdy plastic silverware

Construction

Wooden hollow blocks
Wooden unit blocks
Large cardboard blocks
Wagon or wheelbarrow
Cardboard boxes
Sturdy vehicles: airplanes, boats,
    buses, trucks

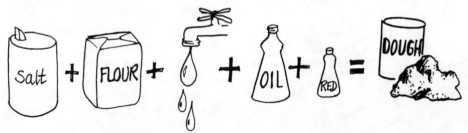

(Play Dough)

Spatulas, potato masher
Pastry-making utensils
Tongue depressors
Cookie cutters
Gelatin molds
Play dishes and food trays
Pipe cleaners, yarn, marbles,
   buttons, leather, feathers
Candles for birthday cakes

(Construction)

Wooden trains and tracks
Miniature persons and animals
Directional map of: center, school,
   play yard, city
Steering wheel mounted on board or
   tree stump
Traffic and safety signs
Old tires and license plates
Hats: police, firefighter, railroad,
   workers, medical
Markers and paper for tickets and
   signs
Interlocking blocks: Lego, Lincoln
   Logs, Bristle, Tinker Toys
Table blocks: Parquetry, design,
   colored cubes

LANGUAGE

Blanket over clothesline, chair or
   cardtable; flashlight for "tent" or
   "hidden cave" play
Dishes for tea party, restaurant or
   pizzeria
Topsy-turvey talking
Sing funny and silly songs: "Bingo,"
   "Wheels on Bus," "Old
   MacDonald"
Play "Ashes, Ashes" and "Pop Goes
   the Weasel" with dolls and stuffed
   animals

Simple hand-clapping rhythms:
   "Miss Mary Mack"
Dance to the Cha-Cha, Hokey Pokey
   or Bunny Hop
Reading books: *Green Eggs and
   Ham, Are You My Mother?, The
   Three Billy Goats Gruff, Millions
   of Cats*
Recite poetry together
Phonograph and children's records
   (or tape recorder)

TRAVEL

Sock puppet
"Diaper bag" for doll: doll blanket,
   bottle, cup, washcloth, plastic
   pants
Rubber or cloth glove with story
   characters on fingers
Metal cookie sheet with magnetic
   shapes
Magic slate with stylus tied to string
Clipboard with paper and tied-on
   pen
Container with top and rubber
   animals
Feltboard inside deep cake pan and
   felt figures
Button, snap or zip doll or book
Cassette of favorite songs or story

The Work Stage: 7 to 10 Years

GROSS MOTOR

Wooden fort climber
Tire and rope climber
Medium-size bicycles
Wagon
Frisbee
Badminton set
Hoops
Jump ropes
Beanbags, wastebaskets, buckets
Ring toss
Sports equipment: soccer, tetherball
Skates
Swim fins and goggles

CONSTRUCTION

Wooden block sets to use on vinyl
    mats (e.g., as maps of school)
Interlocking blocks: Lego, Tinker
    Toys, Lincoln Logs, Construct-o-
    Straws
Erector sets
Table blocks: 3-D, design, colored
    cubes, Parquetry, Blockhead
Simple models to assemble: vehicles,
    human body
Rug-hooking and hobby kits

FINE MOTOR

Barrel of Monkeys: large and small
    types
Garden tools
Canister of buttons to sort and
    classify
Rubber figures with bendable limbs
    for varied positioning
Beanbags
Combination padlocks
Jacks
Blunt-end wooden pick-up-sticks
Jacob's ladder (wooden flip-flop
    stairs)
50+ piece jigsaw puzzles
U.S. map puzzle
Magnets
Binoculars
Small microscope
Gyroscope
Spirograph
Slinky
Patterns for doll clothes and
    furniture

ADULT PARTNER GAMES

Play with double meanings
Sing silly songs with children
Engage in riddling
Tell "Knock-Knock" and animal
    jokes: mice, moose, gorilla,
    elephant
Ask "How do you know?" and
    "What do you think?" questions
Play card and board games with
    children
Play simple team sports with
    children or be the referee
Practice magic tricks with children

SOCIAL-EMOTIONAL

Soft-sculpture boy and girl dolls
Preteen dolls and accessories
Authentic dolls of other countries
Doll houses with furniture
Puppets with wooden or cardboard
    stage
Stand-up paper dolls

MAKE-BELIEVE

Favorite storybook masks and
    costumes
Realistic and adventure theme paper
    dolls
Globe and authentic paper dolls and
    figures from other countries
    (available from UNICEF)
Finger puppets: persons and
    animals
Ventriloquist's doll
Marionettes
Electric trains with tracks, switches,
    signals
Walkie-talkies

ACTIVITY AREAS

Restaurant or Pizzeria

Signs and hats from McDonald's,
    Wendy's, Pizza Hut
Newspaper ads for restaurants
Colored paper uniforms
Paper pads and pencils
Posters of food
Picture (rebus) menus
Magnetic board with letters to make
    signs
Table and chairs
Pitchers, dishes, silverware

Game Center

Card games: UNO, Go Fish,
    character card games
Word games: Boggle, Junior Edition
    of Trivial Pursuit, Jr. Sentence and
    Crossword, Scrabble
Operation
Memory games
Games of chance: Candyland Bingo,
    Bingo
Games of physical skill: Perfection,
    Ring Toss

(Restaurant or Pizzeria)

Tablecloth and sponges
Cash register and play money
Food wrappers and containers
Yellow sponge "fries"
Pizza boards
Play Dough
Mixing bowls
Timers

(Game Center)

Games of skill and strategy:
    Connect-Four, dominoes, checkers,
    Sorry, Parcheesi, Othello, Clue,
    Life, Monopoly

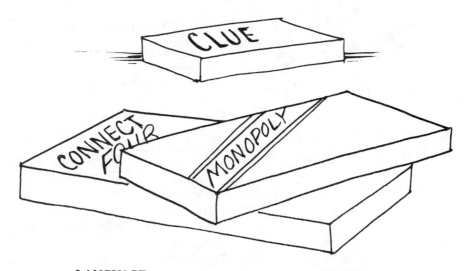

LANGUAGE

Ventriloquist's doll
Marionettes
Sing silly songs and rounds: "The
    Musicians," "The Barnyard Song"
Handclapping rhymes: "Say, Say, My,
    Playmate"
Jump-rope rhymes
"Knock-Knock" jokes, riddles,
    double-meaning word play
Walkie-talkies
Cartoon character books: Peanuts,
    Snoopy, Marmaduke
Books with double meanings: The
    King Who Rained, A Chocolate
    Moose for Dinner, Morris and
    Boris
Children's magazines: Cricket,
    Highlights, Ebony Jr., Ranger Rick,
    Electric Company
Reciting poetry together

TRAVEL

Cassette of favorite jokes and riddles
Cassette of favorite sing-along songs
Clothespin dolls
Finger puppets
Rubber figures with bendable limbs
Jacob's ladder (wooden flip-flop
    stairs)
Etch-a-Sketch
Magnetic Bingo or Tic Tac Toe
Road maps to trace route
Boxed mazes with steel balls
Yarn for cat's cradle
Hairbrush or baster for
    "microphone" interviews
Clipboard of paper or children's
    puzzle pages

Planning and Using Children's Playgrounds

Joe L. Frost

An international authority on playgrounds, Joe L. Frost is Parker Centennial Professor, Department of Curriculum and Instruction, University of Texas at Austin, and U.S. Representative to the International Association for the Child's Right to Play. His most recent books are Children's Play and Playgrounds *(1979) and* When Children Play *(1985).*

Slow but perceptible and growing changes are going on in children's outdoor playgrounds. Fixed, limited-function equipment is being replaced by complex structures that stimulate multiple forms of play. These structures are complemented by a wide range of materials and areas for additional challenge, excitement and learning. The best of these new playgrounds not only provide these advantages, but with proper design and care they are much safer than their early counterparts. Improvement in playscapes is linked to a rapidly growing body of research on play and playgrounds and the success of adventure playgrounds in Europe and contemporary/creative playgrounds in the United States.

The purpose of this article is to illustrate how playgrounds can be improved and used. Several questions are addressed. (1) What should playgrounds contain? (2) How can playgrounds be made safer? (3) What should playgrounds do? (4) How can adults help? Answers to these questions are derived primarily from the University of Texas research represented in the bibliography for this article. The Playground Rating System (p. 66) summarizes views expressed herein and provides a tool for assessment or redevelopment of existing playgrounds or for the development of new ones.

What Should Playgrounds Contain?

The best playgrounds are never finished. Rather, they are constantly changing as new challenges replace old ones and as play equipment and materials are used in fresh combinations. For additional variety, growing things are introduced in nature and garden areas and children create their own structures in the building areas.

Although most items on the playground should be flexible and portable, a major exception is the *superstructure*, a relatively fixed combination of small decks (4 ft. - 6 ft. wide) linked together with challenging apparatus (e.g., steps, clatter bridges, ramps) and providing routes to and from a variety of exercise options or activity devices (e.g., slides, fireman's poles, trapeze bars, climbers). The superstructure combines in one area most of the challenges of a conventional playground comprised of unlinked apparatus. The linkage of play/exercise apparatus is accomplished through use of modular equipment. Using a basic 4 ft. × 4 ft. to 6 ft. × 6 ft. deck as a starting point, up to four activity devices can be attached, one to each of the four sides. Complexity is increased by linking one deck to another with each additional deck offering four new options. The superstructure can be modified to accommodate growing enrollments, changing age groups and developmental needs. Some manufacturers are offering superstructures with considerable flexibility, featuring structures that require no foundations in earth or concrete, decks that can be readily raised or lowered and activity devices that can be moved from deck to deck.

The superstructure is one of two relatively large, fixed structures on modern playgrounds. The second is a swing set. This may be attached to the superstructure or it may be placed in a corner or end of the playground out of the line of direct traffic. Several types are available including conventional swings with pliable strap seats, tire swings mounted on swivels for 360° rotation and movement, and "exerglide" type swings that require upper body exercise for propulsion.

All climbing and moving equipment is installed over sand or equivalent resilient surface for safety and increased playability. Sand is a favorite play material of young children and its advantages far outweigh any problems of sticking to clothing, carrying into classrooms or introducing health risks from animal contamination. Consultation with medical doctors, nurses and playground directors reveals that risks from animal contamination are exaggerated. As one physician put it, "Health risks from chewing on pencils or playing on indoor classroom carpets are greater than playing in sand, which is exposed to natural cleansing agents, wind, rain and sunshine." The play value of sand is enhanced by the provision of a second fluid material, water, and these are further enhanced by providing sand and water play materials—buckets, pans, shovels, strainers. The undersides of well-designed superstructures are favorite sand/water play areas, as well as sites for various dramatic play activities. A crucial principle in design of play environments is illustrated here. Equipment and materials zoned in close proximity can increase challenges, multiply play activities and enhance learning opportunities, while increasing socialization.

A feature of every good playscape is one or more facilities for storing play support materials and wheeled vehicles (tricycles, wagons, wheelbarrows), traffic signs, tools, building materials, benches with vises, sand and water play materials. The storage facility is linked by a ramp to the wheeled vehicle track which poses various challenges (hills, curves, intersections, tunnels), takes children near interesting views (gardens, woods beyond the fence), and links to support structures such as multiple-function play houses that become gas stations, grocery stores or garages. Several important linkages have been discussed: decks to decks, decks to activity devices, superstructures to sand, sand to water, sand and water to sand and water play equipment, storage facility to wheeled vehicle tracks, wheeled vehicle tracks to play houses.

The superstructure is designed primarily for exercise play but, with attention to design and provision of support materials, it also supports dramatic or make-believe play. The dramatic play function of superstructures is further enhanced by placing large dramatic play structures such as boats and cars close to one another. The best location for these items is just outside the superstructure sand area. Cars and boats should be properly stripped: remove upholstery and glass, remove doors, secure the hood and trunk lids, smooth all sharp and jagged parts, and repaint the vehicle. Functional parts such as steering wheels and gear shift levers should remain intact. As dramatic play is initiated in the car or boat and more children become involved, the activity expands to incorporate more than one play structure, frequently including the superstructure. Thus the value of linking the major dramatic play structures with the superstructure becomes obvious.

Unfortunately, some of the most meaningful play activities, from a development and learning perspective, are not supported by adults. Most school administrators reject stripped cars or boats as "unsightly" or "junk yards," but those willing to experiment usually become firm advocates of such play materials. One of the most important forms of play, construction play, is disregarded by most schools and child care centers. A construction area should be available near a storage facility containing tools (high quality saws, hammers, nails, screwdrivers, screws, wrenches, bolts, shovels), scrap lumber (soft wood such as pine, cedar or fir) and workbenches with vises. Construction play must be carefully supervised and basic skills (sawing, nailing) should be *taught* by skilled adults.

Natural features are also important qualities of playgrounds. They should contain nature areas, flat grassy areas for organized games, mounds and hills for challenge and excitement, trees and shrubs for shade and beauty, gardens, animal habitats and live pets that children tend. The prevailing practice of considering such features to be secondary in importance to manufactured exercise devices is a grievous error. The natural features allow a wide range of learning opportunities not available from other playground options.

How Can Playgrounds Be Made Safer?
A great deal has been learned in recent years about playground safety. The most complete data on injuries, fatalities and equipment implicated in injuries and fatalities are available from the National Electronic Injury Surveillance System (NEISS). The Consumer Product Safety Commission has been instrumental in developing guidelines for playground safety. The bibliography includes some of the most important documents on playground safety.

The most common cause of deaths and injuries (70-80 percent of all cases) on public playgrounds (schools and parks) is falling onto hard surfaces (concrete, asphalt). An effective remedy is simple and inexpensive; install 8-10 inches of sand or equivalent resilient surface (pea gravel, bark mulch, shredded tires) under and around all moving equipment (e.g., swings and rotating devices). A retaining border is needed for this material and it must be replenished frequently, particularly in heavy-use areas such as under swings and at slide exits.

Parents are now suing play equipment manufacturers, schools and cities (city parks) for injuries sustained by children on playgrounds. The judgments against these groups are increasing, as are the monetary sums awarded plaintiffs. A common element in a number of lawsuits leading to judgments favoring plaintiffs is the long-term availability of safety guidelines that are commonly violated by manufacturers, equipment installers and playground maintenance personnel.

Examples of injuries and fatalities leading to lawsuits known to the writer include crushing of legs in the undercarriage of revolving mechanisms, amputation of fingers in shearing mechanisms and exposed gears, apparent suffocation from entrapment of the head in guard rails, ruptured body organs and concussions in falls from equipment onto hard surfaces, severe punctures and cuts from exposed bolts, electrocution from accessible electric equipment and drowning in improperly fenced pools of water. This partial list illustrates cases that could have been prevented by adherence to guidelines on design, installation and maintenance.

Entrapment of body parts, particularly the head, is an all too common playground hazard. Hangings are a common cause of fatalities on back-yard playgrounds. These appear to be caused by faulty design, protruding parts and exposed bolts that entrap clothing. Back-yard play equipment may be improperly installed and poorly maintained leading to broken parts, collapse of structure or breaking of swing swivels. Children may be unsupervised for long periods of time in back-yard playgrounds so the child who is accidentally suspended by the head or neck does not have the immediate adult assistance usually available at school playgrounds. Other entrapment areas are frequently found between guard rails on decks, between clatter bridges and decks (bridge cables loosen with use) and between the rungs of ladder-type climbers. Depending on the head dimension of the smallest users, spaces between railings, rungs or angles should not fall between about 4 to 8 inches. Allowance must be made for coat ponchos that can contribute to entrapment.

Most manufacturers design some equipment exceeding reasonable vertical fall heights that can be accommodated by a prescribed resilient surface (e.g., 8-10 inches sand). There appears to be no logical reason for constructing play equipment with climbing heights over 6 ft. - 8 ft. A broad category of hazards includes sharp edges, exposed bolts, protruding elements, pinch points, broken parts and toxic materials. These may be the result of poor design or improper installation or maintenance. All of the above hazards are considered in the Playground Rating System.

What Should Playgrounds Do?

First and foremost, playgrounds should stimulate play, for the values of play are widely documented by researchers and acknowledged by professionals who work with young children. Play is fun, active, spontaneous, self-initiated, challenging, and it is closely linked to learning and development. The playground is merely a stage where children act out, spontaneously and freely, the events that touch their lives and simultaneously develop durable, resilient bodies through movement. In contrast to bad playgrounds, good playgrounds increase the intensity of play and the range of play behavior. More and broader language is produced on good playgrounds and children engage in more "ing" behaviors—running, climbing, sliding, crawling, jumping. Bad playgrounds limit play behavior, restrict language, reduce physical movement and create behavior problems.

Playgrounds should promote learning and development. Play enhances both convergent and divergent problem-solving and it allows better performance on tasks requiring divergent creative thought. Dramatic or symbolic play contributes to a range of developmental virtues including communication, sex-role development, cooperation, perspective-taking ability, creativity, and social and interpersonal problem-solving skills. Skills arising from dramatic play involve the ability to consider various roles simultaneously, to distinguish between literal and non-literal roles and activities, and to perform well on classification and spatial perspective-taking tasks.

The playground should stimulate the senses through a rich array of textures, colors and forms. It should nurture curiosity through a rich ever-changing environment. Portable materials, growing things and live animals are the truly flexible elements of a play environment. Portable materials can be used in an unlimited number of play activities; plants change as they grow and with the seasons; animals grow and change, show their personalities, get sick, give birth, eat and drink. The playground should be fun, a place to escape from routine mental fatigue and boredom, a place to relax and enjoy.

The playground should support the child's basic social, physical and cognitive needs. It should be comfortable, scaled to the child's size, yet physically and intellectually challenging. It should provide for all the forms of cognitive play (exercise, dramatic, construction, organized games) and social play (solitary, cooperative), consistent with the developmental stages of the children. It should encourage and allow interaction among children, materials and adults. The environment must be dynamic, providing graduated challenge—and it must be continuously changing. The best playgrounds are never finished.

Bibliography*

Dean, G. "Motor Behaviors of Kindergarten Children in a Physical Education Class and on a Creative Playground." Doctoral dissertation, The University of Texas at Austin, 1981.

Dempsey, J. "Sociodramatic Play and Children's Cognitive Development." Doctoral dissertation, The University of Texas at Austin, 1985.

Fein, G. "Pretend Play in Childhood: An Integrative Review." *Child Development* 52 (1981): 1095-1118.

Frost, J. "The American Playground Movement." *Childhood Education* 54, 4 (1978): 176-82.

_____. "Toward an Integrated Theory of Play." In *Proceedings of the Brigham Young University's Conference on Music and Child Development*. Reston, VA: Music Educators National Conference, 1985.

_____. "Children's Playgrounds: Research and Practice." In Greta Fein, ed., *The Play of Children: Theory and Research*. Washington, DC: National Association for the Education of Young Children, in press.

Frost, J., and Henniger, M. "Making Playgrounds Safe for Children and Children Safe for Playgrounds." *Young Children* 34, 5 (1979): 23-30.

Frost, J., and Klein, B. L. *Children's Play and Playgrounds*. Austin, TX: Playgrounds International (P.O. Box 33363), 1979, 1984.

Frost, J., and Strickland, E. "Equipment Choices of Young Children During Free Play." *Lutheran Education* 114, 1 (1978): 34-46.

Frost, J., and Sunderlin, S., eds. *When Children Play*. Wheaton, MD.: Association for Childhood Education International, 1985.

Henniger, M. "Free Play Behaviors of Nursery School Children in an Indoor and Outdoor Environment." Doctoral dissertation, The University of Texas at Austin, 1977.

Henniger, M., Strickland, E., and Frost, J. "X-Rated Playgrounds: Issues and Developments." *Journal of Health, Physical Education, Recreation and Dance* (June 1982).

Monroe, M. "A Survey of Title XX Day Care Center Playgrounds in Texas." Doctoral dissertation, The University of Texas at Austin, 1983.

Rubin, K.H., Fein, G., and Vanderberg, B. "Play." In E.M. Hetherington, ed., *Handbook of Child Psychology: Social Development*. New York: Wiley, 1983.

Strickland, E. "Free Play Behaviors and Equipment Choices of Third-Grade Children in Contracting Play Environments." Doctoral dissertation, The University of Texas at Austin, 1979.

Vernon, E. "A Survey of Preprimary and Primary Outdoor Learning Centers/Playgrounds in Texas Public Schools." Doctoral dissertation, The University of Texas at Austin, 1976.

Winter, S. "Toddler Play in an Outdoor Play Environment." Doctoral dissertation, The University of Texas at Austin, 1983.

*Most of the dissertations noted here are published in abbreviated versions in J.L. Frost and S. Sunderlin, eds., *When Children Play*, cited above.

PLAYGROUND RATING SYSTEM*
(Ages 3-8)

Instructions: Rate each item on a scale from 0-5. High score possible on Section I is 100 points, Section II is 50 points and Section III is 50 points, for a possible grand total of 200 points. Divide the grand total score by 2 to obtain a final rating.

Section I. What does the playground contain?

Rate each item for degree of existence and function on a scale of 0-5 (0 = not existent; 1 = some elements exist but not functional; 2 = poor; 3 = average; 4 = good; 5 = all elements exist, excellent function).

_____ 1. A hard-surfaced area with space for games and a network of paths for wheeled toys.

_____ 2. Sand and sand play equipment.

_____ 3. Dramatic play structures (playhouse, old car or boat with complementary equipment, such as adjacent sand and water and housekeeping equipment).

_____ 4. A superstructure with room for many children at a time and with a variety of challenges and exercise options (entries, exits and levels).

_____ 5. Mound(s) of earth for climbing and digging.

_____ 6. Trees and natural area for shade, nature study and play.

_____ 7. Zoning to provide continuous challenge; linkage of areas, functional physical boundaries, vertical and horizontal treatment.

_____ 8. Water play areas, with fountains, pools and sprinklers.

_____ 9. Construction area with junk materials such as tires, crates, planks, boards, bricks and nails; tools should be provided and demolition and construction allowed.

_____ 10. An old vehicle, airplane, boat, car that has been made safe, but not stripped of its play value (should be changed or relocated after a period of time to renew interest).

_____ 11. Equipment for active play: a slide with a large platform at the top (slide may be built into side of a hill); swings that can be used safely in a variety of ways (soft material for seats); climbing trees (mature dead trees that are horizontally positioned); climbing nets.

_____ 12. A large soft area (grass, bark mulch, etc.) for organized games.

_____ 13. Small semi-private spaces at the child's own scale: tunnels, niches, playhouses, hiding places.

_____ 14. Fences, gates, walls and windows that provide security for young children and are adaptable for learning/play.

_____ 15. A garden and flowers located so that they are protected from play, but with easy access for children to tend them. Gardening tools are available.

_____ 16. Provisions for the housing of pets. Pets and supplies available.

_____ 17. A transitional space from outdoors to indoors. This could be a covered play area immediately adjoining the playroom which will protect the children from the sun and rain and extend indoor activities to the outside.

_____ 18. Adequate protected storage for outdoor play equipment, tools for construction and garden areas, and maintenance tools. Storage can be separate: wheeled toys stored near the wheeled vehicle track; sand equipment near the sand enclosure; tools near the construction area. Storage can be in separate structures next to the building or fence. Storage should aid in children's picking-up and putting equipment away at the end of each play period.

_____ 19. Easy access from outdoor play areas to coats, toilets and drinking fountains. Shaded areas and benches for adults and children to sit within the outdoor play areas.

Section II. Is the playground in good repair and relatively safe?

Rate each item for condition and safety on a scale of 0-5 (0 = not existent; 1 = exists but extremely hazardous; 2 = poor; 3 = fair; 4 = good; 5 = excellent condition and relatively safe yet presents challenge).

_____ 1. A protective fence (with lockable gates) next to hazardous areas (streets, etc.).

_____ 2. Eight to ten inches of noncompacted sand (or equivalent) under all climbing and moving equipment, extending through fall zones and secured by retaining wall.

_____ 3. Size of equipment appropriate to age group served. Climbing heights limited to 6-7 feet.

_____ 4. Area free of litter (e.g., broken glass, rocks), electrical hazards, sanitary hazards.

_____ 5. Moving parts free of defects (e.g., no pinch and crush points, bearing not excessively worn).

_____ 6. Equipment free of sharp edges, protruding elements, broken parts, toxic substances.

_____ 7. Swing seats constructed of soft or lightweight material (e.g., rubber, canvas).

_____ 8. All safety equipment in good repair (e.g., guard rails, padded areas, protective covers).

_____ 9. No openings that can entrap a child's head (approximately 4-8 inches). Adequate space between equipment.

_____ 10. Equipment structurally sound. No bending, warping, breaking, sinking, etc. Heavy fixed and moving equipment secured in ground and concrete footings recessed in ground.

Section III. What should the playground do?

Rate each item for degree and quality on a scale of 0-5 (0 = not existent; 1 = some evidence but virtually nonexistent; 2 = poor; 3 = fair; 4 = good; 5 = excellent). Use the space provided for comments.

_____ 1. Encourages Play:
   Inviting, easy access
   Open, flowing and relaxed space
   Clear movement from indoors to outdoors
   Appropriate equipment for the age group(s)

_____ 2. Stimulates the Child's Senses:
   Change and contrasts in scale, light, texture and color
   Flexible equipment
   Diverse experiences

_____ 3. Nurtures the Child's Curiosity:
   Equipment that the child can change
   Materials for experiments and construction
   Plants and animals

_____ 4. Supports the Child's Basic Social and Physical Needs:
   Comfortable to the child
   Scaled to the child
   Physically challenging

_____ 5. Allows Interaction Between the Child and the Resources:
   Systematic storage that defines routines
   Semi-enclosed spaces to read, work a puzzle, or be alone

_____ 6. Allows Interaction Between the Child and Other Children:
   Variety of spaces
   Adequate space to avoid conflicts
   Equipment that invites socialization

_____ 7. Allows Interaction Between the Child and Adults:
   Easy maintenance
   Adequate and convenient storage
   Organization of spaces to allow general supervision
   Rest areas for adults and children

_____ 8. Complements the Cognitive Forms of Play Engaged in by the Child:
   Functional, exercise, gross-motor, active
   Constructive, building, creating
   Dramatic, pretend, make-believe
   Organized games, games with rules

_____ 9. Complements the Social Forms of Play Engaged in by the Child:
   Solitary, private, meditative
   Parallel, side-by-side
   Cooperative interrelationships

_____ 10. Promotes Social and Intellectual Development:
   Provides graduated challenge
   Integrates indoor/outdoor activities
   Involves adults in children's play
   Regular adult-child planning
   The play environment is dynamic—continuously changing

*Joe L. Frost © 1977; revised © 1985.

The Value of Play for Convalescing Children Ages 3 to 12 Years

Doris Lynn Clarke

Doris Lynn Clarke is Assistant Professor in Nursing at Eastern Michigan University. She has worked and taught in pediatric hospitals that include age-appropriate playrooms staffed by child life and early childhood education specialists.

Convalescent play is play that takes place during the recovery phase following illness, surgery or injury. The convalescent play needs of the child may be attended to not only in the hospital, but also at home and in day care, nursery school and school. The trend in health care today is toward a hospital stay that is as brief as possible, with recovery at home using home nursing care, physical therapy, occupational therapy and other supportive services. Further, the aim of pediatric medical and surgical services is to encourage and allow children to return to their usual lifestyle, including preschool and school, as soon as possible.

For the last twenty years, hospital play programs have been developing to meet the play needs of ill children and to prepare them for surgery and invasive diagnostic and treatment procedures. Perhaps most important, play programs help combat the strange, frightening and mysterious environment a hospital projects to children. Special space set aside in hospitals that contain age-appropriate toys and play equipment creates a diminutive environment that feels "safe" to children and provides a therapeutic environment that mediates the passivity, anxiety and boredom hospitalization seems to evoke in children (Poster, 1983).

One value of play is that through its imaginary or quasi-reality property, the player is free to create situations and try them out without fear of repercussion (Vandenberg, 1982). Repetitive play allows children to actively practice and achieve mastery of their environment. Additionally, play has an all-important function in the growth and development of mental health (Noble, 1967). Because a child's body is the primary vehicle through which play is accomplished, illness and subsequent hospitalization can have a significant impact on play experiences (D'Antonio, 1984).

Children in the medical milieu have the same developmental needs for play as all children, with the additional need to adjust and adapt to illness (Azaroff, 1975). Illness may require placing the child in an unfamiliar environment, cause separation from parents and/or family, involve pain and discomfort, and support possible intimation of death. Almost always, it heightens parental anxiety, causing changes in the parent-child relationship (Poster, 1983). According to Petrillo (1980), illness and enforced bedrest cause developmental regression, shortened attention span and decreased ability to concentrate. Preschoolers are particularly at risk for having a diminished opportunity to develop perceptual motor skills and language skills needed for school readiness.

What Are the Benefits of Play for Sick Children?

Play is an especially useful tool for familiarizing children with common hospital materials, equipment and experiences. Play is also useful in seeking cooperation of children for procedures and treatments that are threatening. Play allows for practice of physical skills in a rehabilitative setting. Play allows for ventilation of negative feelings related to confinement or disfigurement such as frustration, anger, rage. Play is retreat; it shuts out the demands of authoritarian adults. Play allows regression in acceptable form. Play is safe. Play is diversion; it actively engages the child, counteracting boredom, isolation, worry, fear, pain (Singer, 1977). Play is fun; children at play are observed to be smiling, laughing, squealing. Even children who are too ill or weak to engage actively in play seem to benefit by watching other children play (Vandenberg, 1982). Finally, play is healing.

Where Should Convalescent Play Be Provided?

Sick children need the opportunity to be in an environment that includes a safe place, appropriate play materials, and adults to direct play who see children as children and not as patients. A therapeutic play environment is an open, relaxed environment that promotes relaxation in children.

A hospital play program ideally exists in an enclosed space (room) that is special for children, safe, insulated from hospital procedures, and separated according to age groups to encourage and support the social aspects of play (Azaroff, 1975). Play space is an important aspect of play. It can be as simple as a cart brought around to children's beds. The child's bed then must be viewed as a place to play and any treatments or procedures should be done elsewhere; for example, a treatment room. Hospital play professionals and volunteers work with parents, using parents to help engage very passive or frightened children in play activity. Play professionals also assist parents, modeling how to engage in age-appropriate play with children and planning play activities the parent and teacher can provide.

When children return to preschool and school programs, they may still have recovery needs that can be met through play activities. In nursery programs, a doctor corner that includes "real" or "real-looking" doctor tools such as stethoscopes, syringes, otoscopes, bandages and hospital clothing helps 3-, 4- and 5-year-olds act out real or imagined experiences that occurred in the hospital. Even though these materials may have been available to the child in a hospital playroom, the child may have felt too ill or been too frightened or intimidated to engage in active dramatic play.

School-age children benefit from the opportunity to share their hospital experience with the class, showing syringes, thermometer covers, medicine cups, all the items they may have collected. Petrillo (1980) suggests having school-age children take pictures, accumulate hospital "collectibles" and make a scrapbook to share with siblings and friends at home and peers at school.

What Kinds of Play Are Appropriate for Convalescing Children?

Physical play involving mobility is critical to young children's sense of well-being. It is natural for a young child to be in motion; although motion may be limited, dictated by the degree of illness, disability or treatment method, physical play should not be restricted as a matter of course. Transportation toys—cars, trains, a steering wheel—provide a child the opportunity to literally be in the driver's seat (Caplan, 1974). Balls, pounding boards, punching bags and big stuffed animals to wrestle are excellent aids for venting frustration and anger. Equipment that provides a rocking, rolling or swinging motion is very soothing to children, especially preschoolers.

Manipulative play, as with blocks, allows young children the opportunity to continue on their natural developmental course. It provides stimulation and resources to gain and regain control, to master and re-master the environment, to gain and regain lost developmental skills. Manipulative play provides opportunity for both imitation and expressive behavior with objects. It also improves strength and promotes ingenuity and problem-solving (Garvey, 1977).

Tactile unstructured materials such as fingerpaint, clay, water and sand are especially useful for sick children. Fingerpainting is a medium for expressing feelings and mood. The process is one of rhythmic movement, improving eye-hand coordination and cognitive skills related to color, texture and concept of thick and thin, wide and narrow, big and little. Clay has varying degrees of malleability, allowing the medium to be altered to accommodate weak fingers or decreased hand mobility. Clay also lends itself to pounding, tearing, construction and destruction.

All children enjoy water play. Sick children seem especially attracted to the opportunity to control a fluid, non-threatening substance. Children can be observed at a water table in a hospital nursery school endlessly pouring water from one container to another. Water can be provided in any safe container—a dishpan, a baby bathtub or a commercial water table. Water play is more entrancing with such things as pitchers, bowls, funnels, ladles, eggbeaters, fishing poles and bubbles.

Sand play also uses a soothing, natural, unstructured substance. Sand is a substance even children with minimal mobility can control. Children like to hold, shape, manipulate, "feel" the texture and temperature of sand. Children also like to dig, bury, hide and push cars and trucks over sand hills and valleys. They also like to "bake" and "eat" their favorite "foods."

Older school-age children enjoy learning real skills as part of play; for example, weaving, carpentry and carving, all skills that improve self-esteem. They like to build elaborate constructions from Lego's, Erector Sets and Tinker Toys. They also enjoy "scrapcrafting" and "junkstruction" from leftover and expendable hospital supplies.

Dramatic play helps children to reveal to adults their understanding and perception of illness and treatment. Using props and transitional (security) objects, it can be helpful in explaining surgical procedures, test procedures, accidental injury and traumatic events to children. Access to a hospital or doctor corner that contains frequently used instruments such as stethoscopes, otoscopes, syringes, cast cutters and bandages provides a safe way for the child to release anger at health care professionals for what they have done to the child or at parents for what they have allowed to happen.

According to Singer and Singer (1977), children who engage in dramatic/ imaginative play are happier children. They have increased self-awareness, increased imagery skills, increased sensitivity and increased creativity. Opportunities for pretend, make-believe or fantasy play enable children to re-create their world to better understand it. Dramatic play allows rules and constraints imposed by illness, casts, tractions, IV equipment or wheelchairs to be set aside.

Dramatic play is greatly enhanced when play areas include dress-up clothes (especially role-identity hats), a housekeeping corner, a doll corner, a doll house (preferably big enough for the child to enter), mirrors, telephones and puppets. For some children, puppets serve as a mask, making acting more comfortable (Sutton-Smith, 1974). Puppets allow three-dimensional play, providing the opportunity to be producer, director and actor. They also make good companions for children who reject dolls, encouraging speech as well.

A doctor corner—with puppets who can be doctor or nurse or patient, real equipment, expendable hospital supplies, hospital furniture, doll families and soft dolls who can withstand multiple "shots"—augments acting out and promotes desensitization of emotionally charged objects.

Games help children to learn rules and boundaries and to develop leadership. Group games become popular in preschool and continue to be increasingly more popular. Sick children often need the help of adults to be included in groups. Games offer the opportunity for a shared activity—child-to-child, parent-to-child, nurse-to-child. Games allow mastery and promote self-esteem (Sutton-Smith, 1974).

Michael, age 10, is an example of a child who used games to help maintain control. Hospitalized for chemotherapy treatment for leukemia, he had to remain flat in bed after receiving an intraspinal medication. He called for a nurse and, in a plaintive voice, asked her to play checkers. Three games and three roustings of the nurse later, Michael was smiling and laughing.

Artistic expression, especially painting and drawing, are useful tools for expressive behavior. Painting improves fine motor skills and specifically serves as a projective tool. Painting is an unstructured task that has no right or wrong. It allows children to reveal thoughts and feelings they cannot verbally express.

Television is frequently used as a convalescent play activity in hospitals and at home. In measured amounts, it offers entertainment and relief from boredom and helps to distract children who are in pain or anxious. Television, however, promotes passivity as does illness. Play that actively engages the child is more therapeutic and more healing for convalescing children.

Play is a valuable tool that helps children to cope with the frightening and mysterious aspects of illness, injury, medical treatment and hospitalization.

References

Azaroff, P., and Flegal, S. *A Pediatric Play Program*. Springfield, MA: Charles C. Thomas, 1975.

Caplan, F., and Caplan, T. *The Power of Play*. Garden City, NY: Anchor Press, 1974.

D'Antonio, I. "Therapeutic Use of Play in Hospitals." *Nursing Clinics of North America* 19 (1984): 351-59.

Garvey, C. *Play*. Cambridge, MA: Harvard University Press, 1977.

Noble, E. *Play and the Sick Child*. London: Faber and Faber, 1967.

Petrillo, M., and Sanger, S. *Emotional Care of Hospitalized Children*. Philadelphia: Lippincott, 1980.

Poster, E. "Stress Immunization: Techniques To Help Children Cope with Hospitalization." *Maternal-Child Nursing Journal* 12 (1983): 119-31.

Singer, D., and Singer, J. *Partners in Play*. New York: Harper and Row, 1977.

Sutton-Smith, B., and Sutton-Smith, S. *How To Play with Your Children*. New York: Hawthorn Books, 1974.

Vandenberg, B., and Kielhofner, G. "Play in Evolution, Culture, and Individual Adaptation: Implications for Therapy." *The American Journal of Occupational Therapy* 36 (1982): 20-28.

Helping the Abused Child Through Play

Emily Jean McFadden

Emily Jean McFadden is Associate Director of the National Foster Care Projects, Eastern Michigan University. She has a social work practice background in child protection and as a therapist for abused children and their families.

THE ABUSED CHILD: A CASE EXAMPLE

Timmy clumsily tiptoed away from the play group, picking up a teddy bear and baby bottle. He glanced at the teachers and scanned the classroom, then quietly crawled under the table, turning his back on his playmates. The teacher's aide noted Timmy's withdrawal and knelt on the floor to observe.

Timmy's face was blank, his eyes lowered. He huddled stiffly with knees folded under him. His fingers fluttered and probed over the teddy bear, poking its eyes, twisting and jerking its paws. Timmy bent over and bit the teddy bear's ears. "Bad teddy," he mumbled, "you're no good. I'll show you who's boss." He slapped the teddy, then grabbing both paws slammed the bear face down into the rug. Then Timmy picked up the baby bottle, shook it and rammed it between the teddy's legs. "This is our secret," he said.

The staff had been puzzled about Timmy for several weeks. He was a quiet, withdrawn 5-year-old who did not engage in play with the others. He seemed mistrustful of adults and usually backed away a step or two when people got close to him. He was not well coordinated, and his speech was babyish. Several staff had been concerned about Timmy's immature development, but because he was quiet, compliant and tended to withdraw, they had focused more on the other children with more obvious problems.

Like thousands of other children, Timmy is an abused child whose development has become frozen as a reaction to trauma. Timmy's play demonstrated the anxiety about touching, the aggression, the damaged body ego and the diminished self-esteem of the abused child. His play was both an attempt to master the fear and pain of his victim role and a cry for help. On observing his play, the alert teacher's aide began to suspect the possibility of physical, emotional or sexual abuse, and initiated intervention to protect Timmy and help his family.

Timmy displayed many behavioral indicators of abuse. They were:

- Timmy was aggressive and abusive to his teddy.
- He verbalized abusive statements in play.
- He attempted to insert the baby bottle between the teddy's legs.
- Attention to the toy's genital area appeared to be more than an expression of curiosity at age 5.
- He showed developmental lag in motor coordination and speech.

- He did not display feelings. His affect was bland; he was hypervigilant and compliant.
- He backed away when people got close to him.
- He talked about "our secret" to his teddy bear. Abused children typically feel the need to keep secrets.

EFFECTS OF MALTREATMENT ON DEVELOPMENT

The child who has experienced parental maltreatment may show developmental lag, or other effects of the abuse, in various developmental spheres:

Physical Development

The abused child has a damaged body ego. Some children adapt to pain by disconnecting from tactile sensation. Such children can be seen hurting themselves, by banging into doorways or falling, with little emotional reaction. They need to learn to feel safe in their own skin. The child's motor coordination may be poor, or mastery of new skills may be limited by broken bones, healing fractures or physical lethargy related to neglect. The child may have learned not to engage in spontaneous activity as an adaptive maneuver to ward off parental abuse.

Emotional Development

The abused or neglected child has difficulty in trusting parents and other adults. Because of damage to the physical sense of self, the child's self-concept is negative. Maltreated children frequently blame themselves for the abuse and internalize parental messages that they are "bad" or "no good." The child often feels responsible for taking care of the parent or younger siblings, an overwhelming task that dooms the child to chronic failure. Although some abused children are aggressive and display obnoxious and provocative behavior, the majority are compliant, self-effacing and withdrawn. They lack spontaneity in expression of feelings, and their affect is bland or depressed.

Social Development

Low self-esteem and inability to trust are often manifested in difficulties with relationships. The child may adopt a stance of frozen watchfulness toward the world, being excessively alert to potential dangers by constantly scanning the environment and monitoring the behavior of adults. Different children adapt in different ways. Some typical patterns follow:

- *The caretaker* is a child who protects him or herself by reversing roles with adults, becoming a parental figure to own parents or teachers. The caretaker is too helpful, too eager to please, and assumes too much responsibility for events.
- *The scapegoat* expects to be treated in an abusive way and to be blamed for whatever goes wrong in the home or classroom. The child has often developed subtle ways to claiming negative attention.
- *The provoker*, like the scapegoat, expects to be treated in a punitive manner. The provoker, however, overtly sets up sequences of negative interactions, perhaps as a way of testing adults or "getting it over with." The provoker is

likely to initiate aggressive interactions by spitting, kicking, biting or punching a caregiver. Some children are stimulated by the arousal state ensuing from parental punishment and seek to repeat this form of gratification.

- *The sexual victim* may have learned inappropriate behaviors as a way of obtaining parental affection or attention. The child may reenact such behaviors with other adults, startling them by touching or stroking their genitals or giving intense hugs and kisses. With other children or in play, the child may display sexualized behaviors and language and assume the role of either the aggressor or victim.

- *The hider* may have learned early to withdraw from tense situations, using isolation as a means of self-protection. Typically, the hider is a very lonely child who shrinks from social contact or suddenly disappears from view if an interaction becomes intense.

Cognitive Development

The effects of maltreatment are evident in the areas of cognitive functioning for abused children. "Well over half of abused children will have significant neuro-development or psychological problems which need attention. Mental retardation, learning disorders, perceptual-motor dysfunction, cerebral palsy and impaired speech and language are among the most common developmental delays and deficits to be found" (Martin, 1976, p. 275). Significant damage to the brain or central nervous system can occur as a result of a child being shaken or receiving a blow to the head. The abused child is likely to display behavior that is dubbed as "hyperactive" or "hyperkinetic." A delay or distortion in speech may mean that the child has learned it is safer not to talk or express feelings.

THE CHILD IN CRISIS: MANIFESTATIONS IN PLAY

A major concern of people who work with children is how to distinguish the abused child from the child who is in crisis for other reasons such as parental illness, divorce or separation. Generally speaking, *abuse may be suspected when the types of developmental lag or dysfunction mentioned above are combined in play with themes of fear and aggression.* Children typically use play to master fears of separation. The games of "Peek-a-Boo" for infants, "Hide-and-Seek" for older children, and doll play involving packing bags, going away and taking naps for preschool-age children are all attempts to master fears of separation through play. When the child is in crisis due to real or impending separations from parents, the play is likely to reflect the theme of separation without involving violence. The abused child is more likely to demonstrate play behavior that combines themes of fear and aggression. One looks for a configuration of signals to suggest abuse, not an isolated play incident.

The sexually abused child's play exhibits knowledge and activity beyond that expected for the child's age and stage of development. While the child in crisis may exhibit curiosity about the genital areas of dolls and toys, the sexually victimized child may simulate intercourse between two dolls, or attempt to insert objects in the genital area of the stuffed animal or "baby." The sexually abused child may masturbate with toys or use a vocabulary of sexual words that are unusually precocious.

The Normal Child in Crisis . . . plays spontaneously and freely	The Abused Child . . . plays in a constricted manner, scans the environment for danger, seems to need adult permission to play
plays in the open	may hide to play
plays to master fear of separations	plays to master fears of pain and retribution in addition to fear of separation
displays aggression toward inanimate objects (trucks, Play Dough)	displays aggression and violence with toys that represent people or loved objects (teddy bears, dolls)
can express anger, sadness through play	is more likely to conceal anger and other feelings, which then erupt through play
displays sexual curiosity, knowledge and language appropriate to age group in play	displays precocious or inappropriate knowledge of sexual issues in play
is more likely to seek support and reassurance from adult figures	is less likely to seek support, appears untrusting, may flinch or wince when approached

The child who is in a family crisis, but is not being abused, will express stress and anxiety in slightly different ways. The child's anxiety is tied to fear of separation, while the abused child's anxiety is linked to the fear of pain as well as the fear of separation. The non-abused child might say in doll play, "I'm going to leave you and go to the hospital to find another baby," whereas the abused child might strike the doll and say, "You're very bad, I'll send you away" or "You're really going to get it next time."

OBSERVATION OF THE CHILD'S PLAY

When observing the play of an abused child, one should keep in mind that the child's overall development may lag, with several deficits in the specific areas mentioned earlier. Thus the quality of the play is often primitive and less complex than that of the child's age group. The play may be the child's only avenue to express or master the difficulties of his or her young life. The play of the abused child may actually be a straightforward representation of the child's troubles.

The written observation of the child at play should include a description of the materials chosen and the manner in which the child chose the toys or materials. It should objectively describe the child's behaviors and words. The observer should attempt to note if there are patterns in the play that are repeated and be alert for the following themes: anxiety, punishment, aggression, keeping secrets, sexual activity or words, and mistrust of adults.

USING PLAY TO HELP THE CHILD AND THE FAMILY

It is important to remember that the abused child, whether in the family, foster family or adopted family, is at high risk to be abused again; the child has learned patterns of interacting with adults that make him or her expect this type of parental behavior. Similarly, the abused child in school or play group may be reenacting the precise behaviors that led to the initial abuse.

The opportunity for play is important to the abused child for a variety of reasons:

- Play can "unfreeze" fixated development, enabling a child to begin growing again.
- Play can help to rebuild a damaged body image.
- Play is a medium through which the child can express and master feelings about the abusive situation.
- Play can be an opportunity to rebuild relationships; it can help the child to develop trust.
- Play can be an opportunity for the child to develop new skills and gain a needed sense of self-confidence.

The enrollment of the abused child in play therapy, play group, preschool and other developmental play programs has obvious benefits. "The child will come into contact with adults who are particularly concerned with his development . . . . Activities can be tailored to meet the child's individual needs and he may begin to trust these adults when they are consistently responsive and non-punitive" (Lero and de Rijcke-Lollis, 1980, p. 176).

Often day care, school or nursery school provides both a haven and an opportunity for the child to grow, develop and heal. Children's play therapy or activity groups provide the opportunity for children to express feelings about the trauma endured. Most children blame themselves for the maltreatment and continue to love their parents despite the genuine fear and pain they may feel. Intervention is needed to help the child cope with these conflicts.

Perhaps the distinction between "therapy" and "other" settings is artificial. Almost all play is therapeutic for the abused child, with the exception of unstructured or unsupervised play that permits the child to act out violence toward other children or pets. In the following section, we will examine several types of play that can be useful in promoting growth for the abused child.

1. Play that enhances the child's body image can combine a number of materials and approaches. Tracing the outline of a child lying down on a long roll of paper is an activity that creates awareness of body boundaries. Tactile sensation can be developed through water play, or by providing the child a number of soft objects to stroke or be stroked with (powder puff, velvet, corduroy, satin). The child can make a book about touching with different kinds of textures pasted in. Play that enhances motor coordination is useful in developing a healthy body image, particularly that play which involves pushing or pressing the body against an object (e.g., crawling through a tunnel or wrapping up in a blanket).

2. Any type of play activity can be trust building if there is an adult close by who gives the child permission for self-expression. For example, an

abused child might be very nervous about staying within the lines in a coloring book. The adult might want to offer reassurance that the child can color outside the lines if desired and there will be no punishment. If the child seems fearful during play, reassurances such as "You won't hurt me" and "I won't hurt you" are useful. Rocking the child in a blanket or sheet while the group sings a soft lullaby can develop trust.

3. Various play activities can protect a child from sexual victimization. With young children, crossing their hands over genitals, breasts and then buttocks can be a game for learning the parts of the body that are covered by the child's bathing suit and shouldn't be touched. Similarly, practicing in role-play skits saying "No" to adults who want to touch can be viewed as a game. Teaching the child phrases such as "This is my body and it belongs to me" or "No one can touch me without my permission" sets the stage for children to play these themes through drawing, puppet play and doll play.

4. There are a number of ways in which play can help children to master feelings about abuse. One way is to allow the child to enact or represent the incident through doll play or drawing, and then later help the child create a new doll play or drawing that shows how people can get along. Only a skilled therapist should help a child "uncover" these situations. If a child chooses to play out such incidents, however, one should allow this expression. Children can be taught to handle pets and toys gently. The adult might sit next to the child holding a bunny and talk about how bunnies need soft touches, just as children need soft touches. It is important to remember that the child may have to unlearn an identification with the aggressor, and is capable of inflicting pain on a pet or another child. Adult modeling can be crucial in helping the child to develop empathy.

5. For those children who have been separated from their parents through foster care placement, play can be a useful way of coming to terms with separation trauma. As the child moves through stages of grief—shock, denial, protest, anger, despair, depression and acceptance—play can be a vehicle for expressing the overwhelming feelings and for allowing a smooth progression through the stages, so that the child does not become "stuck" at the stage of denial or anger. Some activities help the child learn that people do come back. Games having to do with hiding, such as "Hide the Keys" or "Hide-and-Seek," can provide reassurance to the child that the lost will be found.

6. The types of play that enhance self-esteem and sense of identity are almost limitless. It is important to keep in mind that the abused child who is lagging developmentally may well need the toys or play equipment appropriate for a *younger* age group. The child needs tasks that can be mastered easily and in small steps in order to build competence. Abused children have been victims of rigid and high expectation, so that they are always doomed to failure when it comes to accomplishment. Therefore, providing the child with stimulating but "easy" play equipment helps give the child the message that he or she can do well despite all the negative messages

received earlier. To enhance the abused child's identity, play involving the child's name and attributes is useful; for example, a name game, a song or a "book" of drawings that is known as "The Book About Jamie."

An understanding of the types of maltreatment, as well as developmental issues, will help the educator or play therapist to develop play materials, games and situations that meet the unique needs of the abused child. Through appropriate play experiences, the child can begin to grow, feel and trust again.

Postscript

Professionals who work with children have both a legal and a moral obligation to protect the abused child. It is a gut-wrenching experience to watch the pain in an abused child's play or to see the child's bruises. Yet it may be equally frightening to think of reporting abuse and risking a confrontation with an irate parent. It becomes easier to report abuse when one realizes the urgency of obtaining a professional assessment of the degree of danger a child may be in, and when one realizes that reporting brings help to the family.

Abusive parents are not generally "punished." Rather, they are provided help that reduces the risk to the child and enables them to grow as parents.

Professionals and paraprofessionals involved with nurturing the child's development and providing therapeutic play experience should consider themselves part of the child protection team. It is important that they establish open communication with Children's Protective Services.

All states have child protection laws. Typically, reports are made to Children's Protective Services which is a part of the local public welfare or social services department. CPS is usually listed with other emergency numbers in the telephone directory.

References

Bender, B. "Self-Chosen Victims: Scapegoating Behavior Sequential to Battering." *Child Welfare* 6 (1976): 417-22.

Brody, V. "Developmental Play: A Relationship-Focused Program for Children." *Child Welfare* 9 (1978): 591-99.

Eaddy, V., and Gentry, C. "Play with a Purpose: Interviewing Abused or Neglected Children." *Public Welfare* (Winter 1981): 43-47.

Helfer, R., McKinney, J., and Kempe, R. "Arresting or Freezing the Developmental Process." In R. Helfer and H. Kempe, eds., *Child Abuse and Neglect: The Family and Community*. Cambridge: Ballinger, 1976, pp. 65-73.

Kinard, E. "Experiencing Child Abuse: Effects on Emotional Adjustment." *American Journal of Orthopsychiatry* 1 (1982): 82-91.

Lero, D., and De Rijcke-Lollis, S. "Early Childhood Educators: Their Contact with Abused and Neglected Children." *Child Welfare* 3 (1980): 169-78.

Martin, H. *The Abused Child*. Cambridge: Ballinger Publishing, 1976.

Mayhall, P., and Norgard, K. *Child Abuse and Neglect: Sharing Responsibility*. New York: Wiley, 1973.

McFadden, E.J. *Fostering the Battered and Abused Child*. Ypsilanti, MI: Foster Parent Training Project, Eastern Michigan University, 1978.

Children's Books

Freeman, L. *It's My Body* (sexual abuse prevention). Parenting Press, 7750 31st Avenue, N.E., Seattle, WA 98115. 1982.

Williams, J. *Red Flag Green Flag People* (sexual abuse prevention). Rape and Abuse Crises Center of Fargo-Moorhead, P.O. Box 1655, Fargo, ND 58107. 1980.

$\mathcal{B}$ibliography

HISTORY

Froebel, F. *The Education of Man.* New York: Appleton, 1887.

*Hewes, D.W. "Patty Smith Hill: Pioneer for Young Children." *Young Children* 31 (1976): 297-306.

Huizinga, J. *Homo Ludens: A Study of the Play Element in Culture.* Boston: Beacon, 1955.

*Lee, J. *Play in Education.* New York: Macmillan, 1915.

Mergen, B. *Play and Playthings: A Reference Guide.* Westport, CT: Greenwood Press, 1982.

*Osborn, D.K. *Early Childhood Education in Historical Perspective.* Athens, GA: Education Associates, 1980.

Palmer, L.A. *Play Life in the First Eight Years.* Boston: Ginn, 1916.

*Ransbury, M.K. "Friedrich Froebel, 1782-1982: A Re-examination of Froebel's Principles of Childhood Learning." *Childhood Education* 59 (1982): 104-106.

*Snyder, A. *Dauntless Women in Childhood Education: 1856-1931.* Wheaton, MD: Association for Childhood Education International, 1972.

*Spitler, J.A. "Changing Views of Play in the Education of Young Children." Unpublished Doctoral dissertation, Teachers College, Columbia University, New York, 1971.

*Weber, E. *The Kindergarten.* New York: Teachers College Press, 1969.

THEORY AND RESEARCH

Almy, M., ed. *Early Childhood Play.* New York: Selected Academic Readings, 1968.

Barnett, L.A., and Kleiber, D.A. "Concomitants of Playfulness in Early Childhood: Cognitive Abilities and Gender." *Journal of Genetic Psychology* 141 (1982): 115-27.

*Becher, R., and Wolfgang, C. "An Exploration of the Relationship Between Symbolic Representation in Dramatic Play and Art and the Cognitive and Reading Readiness Levels of Kindergarten Children." *Psychology in the Schools* 14 (1977): 377-81.

Berlyne, D.E. "Laughter, Humor and Play." in G. Lindzey and E. Aronson, eds., *The Handbook of Social Psychology,* Vol. 3. Reading, MA: Addison-Wesley, 1969.

Brainerd, C.J. "Effects of Group and Individualized Dramatic Play on Cognitive Development." In D.J. Pepler and K.H. Rubin, eds., *The Play of Children: Current Theory and Research.* Basel, Switzerland: Karger AG, 1982.

*Brown, C.C., and Gottfried, A.W., eds. *Play Interactions: The Role of Toys and Parental Involvement in Children's Development.* Skillman, NJ: Johnson and Johnson, 1985.

*Bruner, J.S., Jolly, A., and Sylva, K. *Play: Its Role in Development and Evolution.* New York: Penguin, 1976.

_____. "Play, Thought, and Language." *Peabody Journal of Education* 60 (1983): 60-69.

*Cazden, C. "Play with Language and Metalinguistic Awareness: One Dimension of Language Experience." *International Journal of Early Childhood* 6 (1974): 12-24.

Chaille, C. "The Child's Conception of Play, Pretending, and Toys." *Human Development* 21 (1978): 201-10.

Cheyne, J.A., and Rubin, K.H. "Playful Precursors of Problem Solving in Preschoolers." *Developmental Psychology* 19 (1983): 577-84.

Christie, J.F. "Effects of Play Tutoring on Young Children's Cognitive Performance." *Journal of Educational Research* 76 (1983): 326-30.

*Christie, J.F., and Johnson, E.P. "Role of Play in Social-Intellectual Development." *Review of Educational Research* 53 (1983): 93-115.

*Cotton, N.S. "Childhood Play as an Analog to Adult Capacity To Work." *Child Psychiatry and Human Development* 14 (1984): 135-44.

*Denotes references useful for STAFF DEVELOPMENT or LENDING LIBRARY.

Dansky, J.L. "Make-Believe: A Mediator of the Relationship Between Free Play and Associative Fluency." *Child Development* 51 (1980): 576-79.

Dewey, J. *Democracy and Education.* New York: Free Press, 1916.

El'konin, D.B. "Symbolics and Its Functions in the Play of Young Children." *Soviet Education* 8 (1966): 35-41.

*Erikson, E.H. *Childhood and Society.* New York: Norton, 1963.

_____. *Toys and Reasons.* New York: Norton, 1977.

Fagot, B.I., and Littman, I. "Stability of Sex Role and Play Interests from Preschool to Elementary School." *The Journal of Psychology* 89 (1975): 285-92.

Fein, G.G. "Echoes from the Nursery: Piaget, Vygotsky, and the Relationship Between Language and Play." In E. Winner and H. Gardner, eds., *Fact, Fiction and Fantasy in Childhood.* San Francisco: Jossey-Bass, 1979.

_____. "Play and the Acquisition of Symbols." In L. Katz, ed., *Current Topics in Early Childhood Education.* New Jersey: Ablex, 1979.

_____. "Pretend Play in Childhood: An Integrative Review." *Child Development* 52 (1981): 1095-118.

_____. "The Self-Building Potential of Make-Believe Play." In T.D. Yawkey and A.D. Pellegrini, eds., *Child's Play.* Hillsdale, NJ: Erlbaum, 1983.

Fein, G.G., ed. *The Play of Children: Theory and Research.* Washington, DC: National Association for the Education of Young Children, 1986.

Feitelson, D. "Cross-Cultural Studies of Representational Play." In B. Tizard and D. Harvey, eds., *Biology of Play.* London: Heinemann, 1977.

*Garvey, C. *Play.* Cambridge, MA: Harvard University Press, 1977.

Golomb, C., and Cornelius, C.B. "Symbolic Play and Its Cognitive Significance." *Developmental Psychology* 13 (1977): 246-52.

*Hartley, R.E., and Goldenson, R.M. *The Complete Book of Children's Play.* New York: Crowell, 1963.

*Hartley, R., Frank, L.K., and Goldenson, R.M. *Understanding Children's Play.* New York: Columbia University Press, 1952.

Herron, R.E., and Sutton-Smith, B., eds. *Child's Play.* New York: Wiley, 1971.

*Hetherington, E.M., Cox, M., and Cox, R. "Play and Social Interaction in Children Following Divorce." *Journal of Social Issues* 35 (1979): 26-49.

Hutt, C., "Exploration and Play." In B. Sutton-Smith, ed., *Play and Learning.* New York: Gardner, 1979.

Johnson, J.E., Ershler, J., and Bell, C. "Play Behavior in a Discovery-Based and a Formal-Education Preschool Program." *Child Development* 51 (1980): 271-74.

Kirschenblatt-Gimblett, B. *Speech Play.* Philadelphia: University of Pennsylvania Press, 1976.

Lamb, M.E. "Father-Infant and Mother-Infant Interaction in the First Year of Life." *Child Development* 48 (1977): 167-81.

*Levy, J. *Play Behavior.* New York: Wiley, 1979.

*Lieberman, J.N. *Playfulness: Its Relationship to Imagination and Creativity.* New York: Academic Press, 1977.

*Lowenfeld, M. *Play in Childhood.* New York: Wiley, 1967.

McLoyd, V.C. "Social Class Differences in Sociodramatic Play: A Critical Review." *Developmental Review* 2 (1982): 1-30.

Mead, G.H. *Mind, Self, and Society.* Chicago: University of Chicago Press, 1934.

*Millar, S. *The Psychology of Play.* Baltimore, MD: Penguin, 1968.

Moore, N.V., Evertson, C.M., and Brophy, J.E. "Solitary Play: Some Functional Reconsiderations." *Developmental Psychology* 10 (1974): 830-34.

Morrison, M., and Gardner, H. "Dragons and Dinosaurs: The Child's Capacity To Differentiate Fantasy from Reality." *Child Development* 49 (1978): 642-48.

Parten, M.B. "Social Participation Among Preschool Children." *Journal of Abnormal and Social Psychology* 27 (1932): 243-69.

*Pellegrini, A.D. "The Relationship Between Kindergartners' Play and Achievement in Prereading, Language, and Writing." *Psychology in the Schools* 17 (1980): 530-35.

Pellegrini, A.D., and Yawkey, T.D. "Children's Play in Early Childhood Education (Symposium)." *Journal of Research and Development in Education* 5-6 (1981): 1-122.

Pepler, D.J. "Play and Divergent Thinking." *Contributions to Human Development* 6 (1982): 64-78.

Pepler, D.J., and Rubin, K.H., eds. "The Play of Children: Current Theory and Research." *Contributions to Human Development* 6 (1982): 64-78.

Phyfe-Perkins, E. *Children's Behavior in Preschool Settings: A Review of Research Concerning the Influence of the Physical Environment.* ERIC Document Reproduction Service, 1979. ERIC NO. ED 168 722.

*Piaget, J. *Play, Dreams, and Imitation in Childhood.* New York: Norton, 1962.

*_____.*The Psychology of Intelligence.* Totowa, NJ: Littlefield and Adams, 1960.

*Piaget, J., and Inhelder, B. *The Psychology of the Child.* New York: Basic, 1969.

Piers, M.W., ed. *Play and Development.* New York: Norton, 1972.

*Reilly, M., ed. *Play as Exploratory Learning.* Beverly Hills, CA: Sage, 1974.

Rubin, K.H. "Nonsocial Play in Preschoolers: Necessarily Evil?" *Child Development* 53 (1982): 651-57.

Rubin, K.H., and Maioni, T.L. "Play Preference and Its Relationship to Egocentrism, Popularity, and Classification Skills in Preschoolers." *Merrill-Palmer Quarterly* 25 (1975): 171-79.

Rubin, K.H., Maioni, T.L., and Hornung, M. "Free Play Behaviors in Middle and Lower Class Preschoolers: Parten and Piaget Revisited." *Child Development* 47 (1976): 414-19.

*Rubin, K.H., Fein, G., and Vandenberg, B. "Play." In E.M. Hetherington, ed., *Handbook of Child Psychology: Social Development.* New York: Wiley, 1983.

Sachs, J. "The Role of Adult-Child Play in Language Development." In K.H. Rubin, ed., *Children's Play.* San Francisco: Jossey-Bass, 1980.

*Saltz, E., and Brodie, J. "Pretend-Play Training in Childhood: A Review and Critique." *Contributions to Human Development* 6 (1982): 97-113.

*Schwartz, J.I. *Metalinguistic Awareness: A Study of Verbal Play in Young Children.* ERIC Document Reproduction Service, 1977. ERIC NO. ED 149 852.

Schwartzman, H.B. *Transformations: The Anthropology of Children's Play.* New York: Plenum, 1978.

Schwartzman, H.B., ed. *Play and Culture.* West Point, NY: Leisure Press, 1980.

Sherrod, L., and Singer, J.L. "The Development of Make-Believe." In J. Goldstein, ed., *Sports, Games, and Play.* Hillsdale, NJ: Erlbaum, 1977.

Shotwell, J.M., Wolf, D., and Gardner, H. "Exploring Early Symbolization: Styles of Achievement." In B. Sutton-Smith, ed., *Play and Learning.* New York: Gardner Press, 1979.

Sinclair, H. "The Transition from Sensorimotor to Symbolic Activity." *Interchange* 1 (1970): 119-26.

*Singer, J., and Singer, D. *Television, Imagination, and Aggression: A Study of Preschoolers.* Hillsdale, NJ: Erlbaum, 1981.

*Smilansky, S. *The Effects of Sociodramatic Play on Disadvantaged Preschool Children.* New York: Wiley, 1968.

Smith, P.K. "A Longitudinal Study of Social Participation in Preschool Children: Solitary and Parallel Play Reexamined." *Developmental Psychology* 14 (1978): 517-23.

Smith, P.K., et al. "Play in Young Children: Problems of Definition, Categorization and Measurement." *Early Child Development and Care* 19 (1985): 25-41.

Smith, P.K., ed. "Children's Play (Symposium)." *Early Child Development and Care* 19 (1985): 1-129.

Smolucha, L.W., and Smolucha, F.C. "Creativity as a Maturation of Symbolic Play." *Journal of Aesthetic Education* 18 (1984): 113-18.

Somers, J.U., and Yawkey, T.D. "Imaginary Play Companions." *Journal of Creative Behavior* 18 (1984): 77-89.

Stevens, P. *Studies in the Anthropology of Play* (Vols. 1, 2 and 3). Cornwall, NY: Leisure Press, 1978.

*Strom, R. "The Merits of Solitary Play." *Childhood Education* 52 (1976): 149-52.

Sutton-Smith, B. "The Role of Play in Cognitive Development." *Young Children* 22 (1967): 361-70.

_____. "A Syntax for Play and Games." In B. Herron and B. Sutton-Smith, eds., *Child's Play.* New York: Wiley, 1971.

_____. "Play as Adaptive Potentiation." In P. Stevens, Jr., ed., *Studies in the Anthropology of Play.* Cornwall, NY: Leisure Press, 1977.

_____. "The Play of Girls." In C.B. Kopp and M. Kirkpatrick, eds., *Becoming Female.* New York: Plenum, 1979.

_____. "Children's Play: Some Sources of Play Theorizing." In K.H. Rubin, ed., *Children's Play.* San Francisco: Jossey-Bass, 1980.

_____. "Piaget, Play, and Cognition Revisited." In W. Overton, ed., *The Relationship Between Social and Cognitive Development.* New York: Erlbaum, 1982.

*Sutton-Smith, B., ed. *Play and Learning.* New York: Gardner, 1979.

Tizard, B., and Harvey, D. *Biology of Play.* Philadelphia: Lippincott, 1977.

Udwin, O., and Shmukler, D. "The Influence of Sociocultural, Economic, and Home Background Factors on Children's Ability To Engage in Imaginative Play." *Developmental Psychology* 17 (1981): 66-72.

Vandenberg, B. "Play, Problem-Solving and Creativity." In K.H. Rubin, ed., *Children's Play.* San Francisco: Jossey-Bass, 1980.

Weininger, O. "Play, Creativity and the Cognitive Unconscious." *Reading Improvement* 18 (1981): 98-107.

*Weisler, A., and McCall, R. "Exploration and Play." *American Psychologist* 31 (1976): 492-508.

Whiting, B., and Edwards, C.P. "A Cross-Cultural Analysis of Sex Differences in the Behavior of Children Aged Three Through Eleven." *The Journal of Social Psychology* 91 (1973): 171-88.

Wilkinson, P.F., ed., *In Celebration of Play.* New York: St. Martin's Press, 1980.

Winnicott, D. *Playing and Reality.* New York: Basic Books, 1971.

Wolf, D., and Grollman, S.H. "Ways of Playing: Individual Differences in Imaginative Style." In D.J. Pepler and K.H. Rubin, eds., *The Play of Children.* Basel, Switzerland: Karger, 1982.

Wolfgang, C.H., ed. "Play and Preschool Aged Child (Symposium)." *Early Child Development and Care* 17 (1984): 1-76.

EDUCATION

Adcock, D., and Segal, M. *Play Together, Grow Together.* White Plains, NY: Mailman Family Press, 1983.

*Almy, M.A. "Child's Right To Play." *Childhood Education* 60 (1984): 350.

Almy, M., et al. "Recent Research on Play: The Perspective of the Teacher." In L.G. Katz, ed., *Current Topics in Early Childhood Education* (Vol. V). Norwood, NJ: Ablex, 1984.

Baker, D. *Understanding the Under-Fives.* London: Evans, 1975.

*Bjorklund, G. *Planning for Play: A Developmental Approach.* Columbus, OH: Merrill, 1978.

*Blau, R., et al. *Activities for School Age Child Care.* Washington, DC: National Association for the Education of Young Children. 1977.

Blocks. Washington, DC: Creative Associates, 1979.

Butler, A.L., Gotts, E.E., and Quisenberry, N.L. *Play as Development.* Columbus, OH: Merrill, 1978.

*Caplan, F., and Caplan, T. *The Power of Play.* Garden City, NY: Anchor, 1974.

Cass, J.E. *Helping Children Grow Through Play.* New York: Schocken, 1973.

Cazden, C. "Play with Language and Metalinguistic Awareness." *International Journal of Early Childhood* 6 (1974): 12-14.

*Chance, P., ed. *Learning Through Play.* New York: Johnson and Johnson, 1979.

Cherry, C. *Creative Play for the Developing Child.* Belmont, CA: Fearon, 1976.

*Coudron, J.M. *Alphabet Puppets.* Belmont, CA: Pitman Learning, 1983.

*Cromwell, L., and Hibner, D. *Finger Frolics.* Livonia, MI: Partner Press, 1976.

Davis, D., Davis, M., Hansen, H., and Hansen, R. *Play Way: Education for Reality.* New York: Holt, 1973.

Dorian, M., and Gullend, F. *Telling Stories Through Movement.* Belmont, CA: Fearon, 1974.

Ebbeck, F.N. "Learning from Play in Other Cultures." *Childhood Education* 48 (1971): 68-74.

Eheart, B.K., and Leavitt, R.L. "Supporting Toddler Play." *Young Children* 40 (1985): 18-22.

*Forman, G.E., and Hill, F. *Constructive Play: Applying Piaget in the Preschool.* Monterey, CA: Brooks/Cole, 1980.

Fowler, W. "On the Value of Both Play and Structure in Early Education." *Young Children* 27, 1 (Oct. 1971): 24-36.

Frank, L.K. "The Role of Play in Child Development." *Childhood Education* 41 (1964): 70-73.

_____. "Play Is Valid." *Childhood Education* 44 (1968): 433-40.

*Frost, J.L., and Klein, B.L. *Children's Play and Playgrounds.* Boston: Allyn and Bacon, 1979.

Frost, J., and Sunderlin, S., eds. *When Children Play.* Wheaton, MD: Association for Childhood Education International, 1985.

*Galda, L. "Playing About a Story: Its Impact on Comprehension." *Reading Teacher* 36 (1982): 52-55.

*Gaston, H. *Kindergarten: Questions and Answers.* Etobicoke Board of Education, 1975.

Geller, L.G. "Linguistic Consciousness-Raising: Child's Play." *Language Arts* 59 (1982): 120-25.

*Gentile, L.M., and Hoot, J.L. "Kindergarten Play: The Foundation of Reading." *Reading Teacher* 36 (1983): 436-39.

*Gordon, I.J. *Baby Learning Through Play.* New York: Macmillan, 1970.

*Gordon, I., et al. *Child Learning Through Child Play.* New York: Macmillan, 1972.

Gray, P., and Chanoff, D. "When Play Is Learning: A School Designed for Self-Directed Education." *Phi Delta Kappan* 65 (1984): 608-11.

Greenlaw, M.J. "Facilitating Play Behavior with Children's Literature." *Childhood Education* 60 (1984): 339-44.

*Griffing, P. "Encouraging Dramatic Play in Young Children." Reprinted in J.S. McKee, ed., *Early Childhood Education 85/86.* Guilford, CT: Dushkin, 1985.

Hartley, R. "Play, the Essential Ingredient." *Childhood Education* 48 (1971): 80-84.

*Hill, D.M. *Mud, Sand, and Water.* Washington, DC: National Association for the Education of Young Children, 1977.

*Hirsch, E.S., ed. *The Block Book* (Rev. ed.). Washington, DC: National Association for the Education of Young Children, 1984.

*Hohmann, M., et al. *Young Children in Action: A Manual for Preschool Educators.* Ypsilanti, MI: High Scope Press, 1979.

*Honig, A.S., and Lally, J.R. *Infant Caregiving.* Syracuse, NY: Syracuse University Press, 1981.

Hooks, W.H., ed. *The Pleasure of Their Company.* Radnor, PA: Chilton, 1981.

House Corner. Washington, DC: Creative Associates, 1979.

*Hymes, J.L., Jr. *Teaching the Child Under Six* (3rd ed.). Columbus, OH: Merrill, 1981.

Jameson, K., and Kidd, P. *Pre-School Play.* New York: Van Nostrand Reinhold, 1974.

Jernberg, A.M. *Theraplay.* San Francisco: Jossey-Bass, 1979.

*Johnson, J. *838 Ways To Amuse a Child.* New York: Gramercy, 1960.

*Kamii, C., and DeVries, R. *Group Games in Early Education: Implications of Piaget's Theory.* Washington, DC: National Association for the Education of Young Children, 1980.

*Karnes, M. *You and Your Small Wonder: Activities for Busy Parents and Babies.* Circle Pines, MN: American Guidance Service, 1982.

_____. *You and Your Small Wonder: Activities for Parents and Toddlers on the Go.* Circle Pines, MN: American Guidance Service, 1982.

*Kritchevsky, S., and Prescott, E. *Planning Environments for Young Children: Physical Space.* Washington, DC: National Association for the Education of Young Children, 1969.

*LeHane, S. *Help Your Baby Learn: 100 Piaget Based Activities for the First Two Years of Life.* Englewood Cliffs, NJ: Prentice-Hall, 1976.

*Lindberg, L., and Swedlow, R. *Early Childhood Education: A Guide for Observation and Participation* (2nd ed.). Boston: Allyn and Bacon, 1980.

*Linderman, C.E. *Teachables from Trashables: Homemade Toys That Teach.* Mt. Rainier, MD: Gryphon, 1979.

*Markun, P.M., ed. *Play: Children's Business.* Wheaton, MD: Association for Childhood Education International, 1974.

Marzollo, J., and Lloyd, J. *Learning Through Play.* New York: Harper and Row, 1972.

*McCoy, E. *The Incredible Year-Round Playbook.* New York: Random House, 1979.

McIntyre, M. "Discovery Through Sand Play." *Science and Children* 19 (1982): 36-37.

McLellan, J. *The Question of Play.* New York: Pergamon, 1970.

*Moffitt, M., and Swedlow, R. "The Dynamics of Play for Learning." In P. Markun, ed., *Play: Children's Business.* Wheaton, MD: Association for Childhood Education International, 1974, pp. 38-44.

Noyes, M. "Sandplay Imagery: An Aid to Teaching Reading." *Academic Therapy* 17 (1981): 231-37.

Nursery School Portfolio. Wheaton, MD: Association for Childhood Education International, 1961.

*Oppenheim, J.F. *Kids and Play.* New York: Ballantine Books, 1984.

Parten, M.B. "Social Participation in Preschool Children." *Journal of Abnormal Social Psychology* 28 (1933): 136-47.

*Pellegrini, A.D., et al. "Saying What You Mean: Using Play To Teach Literate Language." *Language Arts* 60 (1983): 380-84.

Piers, M.W., and Millet-Landau, G. *The Gift of Play.* New York: Walker, 1980.

*Pitcher, E.G., et al. *Helping Young Children Learn* (4th ed.). Columbus, OH: Merrill, 1984.

*Pitcher, E.G., and Schultz, L.H. *Boys and Girls at Play: The Development of Sex Roles.* New York: Praeger, 1983.

*Pratt, C. *I Learn from Children.* New York: Cornerstone Library, 1970.

Provenzo, E.F., and Brett, A. *The Complete Block Book.* New York: Syracuse University Press, 1983.

Provenzo, E.F., and Brett, A. "Creative Block Play." *Day Care and Early Education* 11 (1984): 6-8.

*Reilly, M., ed. *Play as Exploratory Learning.* Beverly Hills, CA: Sage, 1974.

Riley, S.S. "Some Reflections on the Value of Children's Play." *Young Children* 28, 3 (1973): 146-53.

*Scarfe, N.V. "Play Is Education." *Childhood Education* 39 (1962): 117-21.

*Segal, M.M. *The Nova University Play Program: From Birth to 1 Year.* Ft. Lauderdale, FL: Nova University Press, 1974.

*Segal, M.M., and Adcock, D. *Just Pretending: Ways to Help Children Grow Through Imaginative Play.* Englewood Cliffs, NJ: Prentice-Hall, 1981.

Severeide, R.C., and Pizzini, E.L. "What Research Says: The Role of Play in Science." *Science and Children* 21 (1984): 58-61.

Simpson, D., and Alderson, D.M. *Creative Play in the Infants' School.* London: Isaac Pitman and Sons, 1968.

*Singer, D.G., and Singer, J.L. *Partners in Play.* New York: Harper and Row, 1977.

Southern Association on Children Under Six. *Dimensions* (1975): 3.

Sponseller, D. "Play and Early Education." In B. Spodek, ed., *Handbook of Research on Early Childhood Education.* New York: Free Press, 1982, pp. 215-41.

*Sponseller, D., ed. *Play as a Learning Medium.* Washington, DC: National Association for the Education of Young Children, 1974.

Strom, R.D. *Growing Through Play: Readings for Parents and Teachers.* Monterrey, CA: Brooks/Cole, 1981.

Sutton-Smith, B. "The Role of Play in Cognitive Development." *Young Children* 22 (1967): 361-70.

*Sutton-Smith, B., and Sutton-Smith, S. *How To Play with Your Children (And When Not To).* New York: Hawthorne, 1974.

*Sylva, K. "A Hard-Headed Look at the Fruits of Play." *Early Child Development and Care* 15 (1984): 171-83.

Table Toys. Washington, DC: Creative Associates, 1979.

Taylor, B.J. *A Child Goes Forth: A Curriculum Guide for Teachers of Preschool Children.* Provo, UT: Brigham Young University Press, 1985.

*Thibault, J.P., and McKee, J.S. "Practical Parenting with Piaget." *Young Children* 38 (1982): 18-27.

*Tudor-Hart, B. *Toys, Play and Discipline in Childhood.* London: Routledge and Kegan Paul, 1970.

Weininger, O. *Play and Education.* Springfield, IL: Charles C. Thomas, 1979.

Wilkinson, P.F., ed. *In Celebration of Play.* New York: St. Martin's Press, 1980.

*Wolfgang, C.H. *Helping Aggressive and Passive Preschoolers Through Play.* Columbus, OH: Merrill, 1977.

_____. "A Study of Play as a Predictor of Social-Emotional Development." *Early Child Development and Care* 13 (1983): 33-54.

*Wolfgang, C.H., et al. *Growing and Learning Through Play.* New York: McGraw-Hill, 1981.

*Wolfgang, C.H., and Sanders, T.S. "Defending Young Children's Play as the Ladder to Literacy." *Theory into Practice* 20 (1981): 116-20.

Wolfgang, C.H., and Sanders, T. "Teachers' Role: A Construct for Supporting the Play of Young Children." *Early Child Development and Care* 8 (1982): 107-20.

Woodard, C.Y. "Guidelines for Facilitating Sociodramatic Play." *Childhood Education* 60 (1984): 172-77.

Zubrowski, B. "Play as Education in School-Age Day Care Programs." *Day Care and Early Education* 9 (1981): 17-19.

PLAY MATERIALS

Adcock, D., and Segal, M. *Play and Learning.* Ft. Lauderdale, FL: Nova University, 1979.

Allen, A., and Neterer, E. "A Guide to Play Materials." In P.M. Markun, ed., *Play: Children's Business.* Wheaton, MD: Association for Childhood Education International, 1974.

Benjamin, H. "Age and Sex Differences in Toy Preference of Young Children." *Journal of Genetic Psychology* 41 (1932): 417-29.

Butler, A.L., Gotts, E., and Quisenberry, N.L. *Play as Development*. Columbus, OH: Merrill, 1978.

Caney, S. *Toy Book*. New York: Workman, 1972.

*Cataldo, C. *Infant and Toddler Programs*. Reading, MA: Addison-Wesley, 1983.

Davidson, D. *Soft Toys*. Newton, MA: Branford, 1971.

Feenery, S., and Magarick, M. *Choosing Good Toys for Young Children*. Washington, DC: National Association for the Education of Young Children, 1984.

Hewitt, K., and Roomet, L. *Recreational Toys in America: 1800 to the Present*. Burlington, VT: Robert Hull Museum, 1979.

*Hirsch, E., ed. *The Block Book* (Rev. ed.). Washington, DC: National Association for the Education of Young Children, 1984.

Ives, S. *Making Felt Toys and Glove Puppets*. Newton, MA: Branford, 1971.

Johnson, H.M. *The Art of Block Building*. New York: Day, 1933.

Kaban, B. *Choosing Toys for Children from Birth to Five*. New York: Schocken, 1979.

Kawin, E. *The Wise Choice of Toys*. Chicago: University of Chicago Press, 1938.

*Linderman, C.E. *Teachables from Trashables*. Mt. Rainier, MD: Toys 'N Things, 1979.

*Matterson, E.M. *Play and Playthings for the Preschool Child* (Rev. ed.). Baltimore, MD: Penguin, 1967.

McConkey, R., and Jeffree, D. *Making Toys for Handicapped Children*. Englewood Cliffs, NJ: 1981.

Newson, J., and Newson, E. *Toys and Playthings*. New York: Pantheon, 1979.

Pogrebin, L.C. *Growing Up Free*. New York: Bantam, 1980.

Provenzo, E.F., and Brett, A. *The Complete Block Book*. New York: Syracuse University Press, 1983.

*Sutton-Smith, B., and Sutton-Smith, S. *How To Play with Your Children (And When Not To)*. New York: Hawthorne, 1974.

Swan, S.K. *Home-Made Baby Toys*. Boston: Houghton-Mifflin, 1977.

Tronick, E., and Greenfield, P.M. *Infant Curriculum*. Santa Monica, CA: Goodyear, 1980.

Yawkey, T.D., and Trostle, S.L. *Learning Is Child's Play*. Provo, UT: Brigham Young University Press, 1982.

Van Alstyne, D. *Play Behavior and Choice of Play Materials of Preschool Children*. Chicago: University of Chicago Press, 1932.

SPECIAL NEEDS CHILDREN

Baker, B.L., Brightman, A.J., and Blacher, J.B. *Play Skills*. Champaign, IL: Research Press, 1983.

Barnett, L.A., and Fiscella, J. "A Child by Any Other Name . . . A Comparison of the Playfulness of Gifted and Nongifted Children." *Gifted Child Quarterly* 29 (1985): 61-66.

Bleck, R.T., and Bleck, B.L. "Disruptive Child's Play Group." *Elementary School Guidance and Counseling* 17 (1982): 137-41.

Brophy, K., and Stone-Zukowski, D. "Social and Play Behavior of Special Needs and Non-Special Needs Toddlers." *Early Child Development and Care* 13 (1984): 137-54.

Cratty, B.J., and Breen, J.E. *Educational Games for Physically Handicapped Children*. Denver, CO: Love Publishing Co., 1972.

Crawley, S.B., and Chan, K.S. "Developmental Changes in Free-Play Behavior of Mildly and Moderately Retarded Preschool-Aged Children." *Education and Training of Mentally Retarded* 17 (1982): 234-39.

Cunningham, C.C., et al. "Mental Ability, Symbolic Play, and Receptive and Expressive Language of Young Children with Down's Syndrome." *Journal of Child Psychology, Psychiatry and Allied Disciplines* 26 (1985): 255-65.

Federlein, A.C., et al. "Special Education Preschoolers: Evaluating Their Play." *Early Childhood Development and Care* 8 (1982): 107-20.

*Field, T., Roseman, S., DeStefano, L.J., and Koewler, J. "The Play of Handicapped Preschool Children with Handicapped and Non-Handicapped Peers in Integrated and Nonintegrated Situations." *Topics in Early Childhood Special Education* 3 (1982): 28-38.

Gumaer, J. "Developmental Play in Small Group Counseling with Disturbed Children." *School Counselor* 31 (1984): 445-53.

Harvey, S. "Training the Hospital Play Specialist." *Early Child Development and Care* 17 (1984): 277-90.

Higginbotham, D.J., and Baker, B.M. "Special Participation and Cognitive Play Differences in Hearing-Impaired and Normally Hearing Preschoolers." *Volta Review* 83 (1981): 135-49.

Kasari, C., and Filler, J.W. "Using Inflatables with Severely Motorically Involved Infants and Preschoolers." *Teaching Exceptional Children* 14 (1981): 22-26.

Levy, L., and Gottlief, J. "Learning Disabled and Non-Learning Disabled Children at Play." *Remedial Special Education* 5 (1984): 43-50.

Li, A.K.F. "Play and the Mentally Retarded Child." *Mental Retardation* 19 (1981): 121-26.

Moran, J.M., and Kalakian, L.H. *Movement Experiences*. Minneapolis, MN: Burgess, 1977.

Newson, E., and Hipgrave, T. *Getting Through to Your Handicapped Child*. New York: Cambridge University Press, 1982.

Odom, S.L. "Relationship of Play to Developmental Level in Mentally Retarded Preschool Children." *Education and Training of Mentally Retarded* 16 (1981): 136-41.

Riquet, C.B., et al. "Symbolic Play in Autistic, Down's, and Normal Children of Equivalent Mental Age." *Journal of Autism and Developmental Disabilities* 11 (1981): 439-48.

Rogers, S.J., and Puchalski, C.B. "Development of Symbolic Play in Visually Impaired Young Children." *Topics in Early Childhood Special Education* 3 (1984): 57-63.

Roswal, G.M. "Camp HELP: Serving the Multihandicapped Through Play." *Journal of Physical Education, Recreation, and Dance* 54 (1983): 42-44.

Schleifer, M.J. "John Doesn't Know How To Play: Play and the Grade-School Child." *Exceptional Parent* 13 (1983): 33-38.

Terrell, B.Y., et al. "Symbolic Play in Normal and Language-Impaired Children." *Journal of Speech and Hearing Research* 27 (1984): 424-29.

Ungerer, J.A., and Sigman, M. "Symbolic Play and Language Comprehension in Autistic Children." *Journal of American Academy of Child Psychology* 20 (1981): 318-37.

Wehman, P. *Helping the Mentally Retarded Acquire Play Skills*. Springfield, IL: Thomas, 1977.

*Widerstrom, A. "How Important Is Play for Handicapped Children?" Reprinted in J.S. McKee, ed., *Early Childhood Education 85/86*. Guilford, CT: Dushkin, 1985.

PLAY THERAPY

Axline, V. *Play Therapy*. Boston: Houghton–Mifflin, 1947.

*_____. *Dibs: In Search of Self*. Boston: Houghton–Mifflin, 1964.

Moustakas, C. *Psychotherapy with Children*. New York: Harper and Row, 1959.

_____. *Children in Play Therapy*. New York: Aronson, 1973.

Moustakas, C., ed. *The Child's Discovery of Himself*. New York: Ballantine, 1974.

Schaefer, C.E. *Therapeutic Use of Child's Play*. New York: Aronson, 1976.

_____. "Play Therapy." *Early Child Development and Care* 19 (1985): 95-108.

Yawkey, T.D., and Pellegrini, A.D., eds. *Child's Play and Play Therapy*. Lancaster, PA: Technomic, 1984.

PLAY GROUPS

Broad, L. *The Play Group Handbook*. New York: St. Martin's Press, 1974.

Ferri, E., and Niblett, R. *Disadvantaged Families and Playgroups*. Atlantic Highlands, NJ: Humanities Press, n.d.

Lucas, J., and McKennel, V. *The Penguin Book of Playgroups*. Baltimore, MD: Penguin, 1974.

*Sylva, K., Roy, C., and Painter, M. *Childwatching at Playgroup and Nursery School*. Ypsilanti, MI: High Scope Press, 1980.

*Winn, M., and Porcher, M.A. *The Playgroup Book*. Baltimore, MD: Penguin, 1969.

GAMES

Arnold, A. *The World Book of Children's Games*. Greenwich, CT: Fawcett, 1972.

Avedon, E.M., and Sutton-Smith, B. *The Study of Games*. New York: Wiley, 1971.

*Ferretti, F. *The Great American Book of Sidewalk, Stoop, Dirt, Curb, and Alley Games*. New York: Workman, 1975.

*Fluegelman, A., ed. *The New Games Book*. San Francisco, CA: Headlands Press, 1976.

Michaelis, B., and Michaelis, D. *Learning Through Noncompetitive Activities and Play*. Palo Alto, CA: Education Today, 1977.

Opie, I., and Opie, P. *Children's Games in the Street and Playground*. London: Oxford University Press, 1969.

Orlick, T. *The Second Cooperative Sports Games Book*. New York: Pantheon, 1982.

Sutton-Smith, B. *The Developmental Psychology of Children's Games*. Baltimore, MD: Penguin, 1973.

When Children Play

Proceedings of the International Conference on Play and Play Environments

Joe L. Frost and Sylvia Sunderlin, Editors

365 pp., illustrated
ISBN 0-87173-107-X
$29.50 ACEI Members
$35.00 Nonmembers

"Here is a book that lends sound, scholarly support to what many of us have assumed all along: that play and childhood go together. . . . The volume is a valuable, comprehensive resource that does justice to the editors' stated goals, the first being 'We should seek to understand play.'" — Eve Burton, Parent Educator, Montgomery County Public Schools, MD

"Play is universal, knowing no national or cultural boundaries," writes coeditor Joe L. Frost in his introduction to this comprehensive resource. "It is peculiar to all ages and all races, subject to description yet defying definition; essential to the development of thought and language, yet neither; central to the transmission of culture, yet transcending culture."

How does play affect language development? What kinds of playgrounds attract children and which are inappropriate or extremely dangerous? What types of play and play environments are created in other countries? How can playgrounds be developed using plants and trees? To allow for experimentation with music? To enable hospitalized children the full range and benefits of play? How do children themselves describe their play? The 47 papers in this book address these questions as they explore the vastly unexplored terrain of play:

Part I: Understanding Play
Part II: Play, Learning and Development
Part III: How Children Use Playgrounds
Part IV: Trends in Designing and Developing Playgrounds
Part V: Indoor Play Environments and Play Materials
Part VI: The Role of Adults in Promoting Play
Part VII: Play as an Assessment Tool

This 365-page book is copiously illustrated with playground designs, tables and diagrams, reflecting the broad scope of the various discussions of "the play of children and the environments for play," which poured out of that comprehensive conference.

To order write: ACEI Publications, Dept. PW, 11141 Georgia Ave., Suite 200, Wheaton, MD 20902. Add postage/handling charges: 1-2 copies, $1.00 (minimum); 3-6, $1.50; 7-10, $2.00. No billed orders under $30.00 unless on authorized purchase order forms.